Resources and Counseling for the Arts'

Handbook for Minnesota Artists

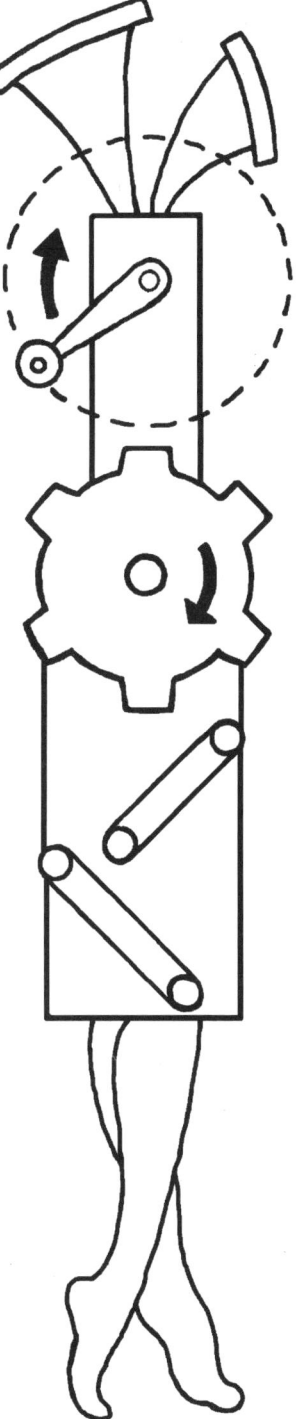

still latest edition—
checked 06/08 JK

Handbook For Minnesota Artists
Fourth Edition

copyright © 2000 Resources and Counseling for the Arts
First Edition, October 1992, Fourth Edition, April 2000

ISBN 0-70003-0-7 12.00
Editor: Fred Schmalz
Research Coordinators: Kate Nordstrum, Kerry Sheehy
Artwork: Stephen Rue
First and Second Edition Editor: Robin Edgerton
Third Edition Editor: Laurie Wolfson
RCA Staff: Joan Wells, Chris Osgood, Christine Deger, Emily Johnson, Fred Schmalz, Kate Nordstrum.

 This publication can be produced in alternate formats for people with visual impairments.

For additional copies contact:
Resources and Counseling for the Arts
308 Prince St. Suite 270
St. Paul, MN 55101-1437
Phone: 651-292-4381
Fax: 651-292-4315
TTY: 651-292-3218
email: info@rc4arts.org
Website: www.rc4arts.org *— no longer valid address 06/08*

Other publications available from RCA include:
Grants: A Basic Guide to Grants for Minnesota Artists
Exhibit: A Basic Guide to Gallery and Exhibition Spaces in Minnesota
Space: A Basic Guide to Performance and Rehearsal Spaces in Minnesota
Art Work: Opportunities in Arts Administration

Grants, Exhibit, and *Space* are joint projects of RCA and the Minnesota State Arts Board. The publications are free and available by contacting RCA or the Minnesota State Arts Board. Downloadable versions of *Grants, Exhibit,* and *Space* available at Minnesota State Arts Board website (www.arts.state.mn.us).

Note:

Handbook for Minnesota Artists, Fourth Edition, is a project of Resources and Counseling for the Arts (RCA), a source of management information and training for independent artists and small to mid-sized cultural organizations. Our services are designed to improve the professional competence and confidence of artists, art groups, and nonprofit organizations. RCA offers friendly and affordable training, information, consultation, career counseling and referrals on business and professional development issues as they apply to the arts and related fields.

Special funding for the Handbook has been provided by:
Semisonic
Medtronic Foundation

Thanks to:
Abdo & Abdo
Oppenheimer Wolff & Donnelly, L.L.P.
Arts & Entertainment Law Section of the Minnesota State Bar Association
Faegre & Benson, L.L.P.
Fish & Richardson, P.C., P.A.
Fredrikson & Byron, P.A.
Minnesota Film Board
Rider Bennett Egan & Arundel, L.L.P.
City of Saint Paul Office of Cultural Development
Spence Olson, P.L.L.C.
Begley Law Offices, P.A.
Kenneth L Kunkle, Attorney at Law
Noiseland

Introduction

Where can I get funding for my film company's new project? Who can tell me about health care options for me and my family? I'm new to town; is there a group that works with area dancers and choreographers? RCA's *Handbook for Minnesota Artists* was created to answer questions that area artists and self-employed creative people often ask.

Handbook for Minnesota Artists is meant to be a first stop in the search for information, helpful people and practical solutions – a tool to manage immediate problems and contribute to long-term career building. It is our intention to include contact information for organizations that are logical "first steps" in collecting useful information on arts and living issues for creative people in Minnesota. For example, in the **Grants** section, you will find entries of organizations which provide resources on grants, such as the Minnesota Council on Foundations, the Minnesota State Arts Board and RCA. You will not find a listing of all the funding sources available to Minnesota artists.

The book is divided into common areas of interest for artists. For example, the **Health & Human Services** section contains insurance options, sliding-scale and discounted care options for lower-income artists, alternative health care, occupational health and safety information, etc. In most cases there will be more than one resource to investigate. Most organizations listed are nonprofit or publicly funded.

In each entry, we provide contact information, indicate the organization's services, its educational offerings, and any fees attached to membership or programming.

Our intention is to make the *Handbook for Minnesota Artists* a useful tool for artists throughout the state. We look forward to your feedback and suggestions on how we can improve it.

Table of Contents

Information for All Artists — 1

- General Arts Organizations and Resources — 2
- Arts Associations — 7
- Art Councils — 10
- Community Art Centers — 15
- Cultural Centers — 20
- Community Television Broadcast — 24
- Community Newspapers — 24
- Arts Education — 26
- Public Art — 30
- Helpful Websites — 31

Information by Art Form — 32

- Resources for Visual Artists — 33
- Watercolor — 35
- Cartooning — 36
- Sculpture — 37
- Wood & Metal — 38
- Design — 40
- Film & Video — 43
- Photography — 45
- Website Construction — 47
- Crafts — 48
- Ceramics — 49
- Fiber Arts & Textiles — 50
- Music — 55
- Theater & Performance — 61
- Dance — 63
- Storytelling — 65
- Writing & Literature — 66
- Book & Paper Arts — 69

Grants, Funds & Employment   71

   Artist Grants & Fellowships   72
   Artist Residencies   77
   Artist Loans   79
   Small Business Loans   79
   Housing Loans   80
   Emergency Funds   83
   Employment   86

Business & Legal Services   89

   Credit Counseling   90
   Financial Management   91
   Accounting   93
   Government Services   94
   Copyright & Patent   95
   Advocacy   96
   Mediation   98
   Legal Assistance   99

Health & Human Services   100

   Housing & Studio Space   101
   Health Insurance   102
   Sliding Scale Medical   106
   AIDS Info and Services   110
   Occupational Health & Safety   111
   Alternative Forms of Healthcare   112
   Utilities Assistance   113
   Crisis Intervention   114
   Food   117
   Disability Services   118
   Childcare   120

Index   123

Information For All Artists

General Arts Organizations and Resources	2
Arts Associations	7
Art Councils	10
Community Art Centers	15
Cultural Centers	20
Community Television Broadcast	24
Community Newspapers	24
Arts Education	26
Public Art	30
Helpful Websites	31

For All Artists – General Arts Organizations and Resources

General Arts Organizations and Resources

American Council for the Arts Book Catalog

American Council for the Arts, Dept. 32, 1 53rd St. E, New York, NY 10022
Phone: 212-223-2787   Website: www.artsusa.org
Fax: 212-980-4857
Toll-Free: 800-321-4510

Services: The Council offers an online order service for publications on the business as well as the political and intellectual side of the arts. Publications include many marketing, management, career, and resource books.

Artists of Minnesota

204 Second St. E, Hastings, MN 55033

Services: Artists of Minnesota is a nonprofit organization dedicated to promoting practice and interest in the creative arts among the people of Minnesota. It publishes *The Palette News* six times per year, holds seasonal shows, offers workshops, and informs members of local arts happenings.

Fees: $20/regular annual membership.

Arts Midwest

528 Hennepin Ave. S, Suite 310, Minneapolis, MN 55403
Phone: 612-341-0755   Email: general@artsmidwest.org
Fax: 612-341-0902   Website: www.artsmidwest.org
TTY: 612-341-0901

Services: Arts Midwest is a nonprofit regional organization connecting the arts to audiences throughout Illinois, Indiana, Iowa, Michigan, Minnesota, North Dakota, Ohio, South Dakota, and Wisconsin. Its mission is to enable individuals and families throughout the midwest to share in and enjoy the arts and cultures of our region and world.

Education: Annual arts conference.

For All Artists – General Arts Organizations and Resources

College Art Association

275 7th Ave., New York, NY 10001
Phone: 212-691-1051 Email: nyoffice@collegeart.org
Fax: 212-627-2381 Website: www.collegeart.org

Services: CAA promotes excellence in scholarship and teaching in the history and criticism of the visual arts, and in creativity and technical skill in the teaching and practices of art. Member benefits include group rates on health, disability, life, and other insurance plans, as wells as access to all CAA journals and publications, use of their Annual Conference job placement service, and eligibility for awards and travel grants.

Fees: Membership fees are income-based.

COMPAS

304 Landmark Center, 75 Fifth St. W, St. Paul, MN 55102
Phone: 651-292-3249 Email: compas@migizi.com
Fax: 651-292-3258 Website: www.compas.org
Toll-free: 800-826-6012

Services: COMPAS provides funds for community art projects, and offers many artist-in-residence programs in schools and other community sites across the state. There is a focus on diverse cultural programming, support, and community-building.

Fees: Vary.

The Gold Book

Prime Publications, Inc., 318 Groveland Ave., Minneapolis, MN 55403
Phone: 612-872-7700 Email: info@primepub.com
Fax: 612-872-0121
Toll-Free: 888-590-3965

Services: *The Gold Book* is an annual directory of advertising, publishing, communications, and creative service industries in the seven-county Metropolitan area.

For All Artists – General Arts Organizations and Resources

Intermedia Arts

2822 Lyndale Ave. S, Minneapolis, MN 55408
Phone: 612-871-4444　　　　Email: allstaff@IntermediaArts.org
Fax: 612-871-6927　　　　　Website: www.IntermediaArts.org

Services: Intermedia Arts supports and presents visual, performance, video, film, and interdisciplinary art and offers a broad range of services to artists.

Education: classes and workshops for artists, youth, and educators.

JuxtaPosition Arts

280 Second Ave. N, Suite 201, Minneapolis, MN 55401
Phone: 612-374-1418　　　　Website: www.juxtaposition.org
Fax: 612-374-1419

Services: Juxtaposition Arts is a nonprofit visual arts organization engaging audiences through youth studio arts programs and neighborhood art events.

Education: Community Arts Partnership, Studio Arts Program, Community Murals, and short term workshops.

Management Assistance Project (MAP) for Nonprofits

2233 University Ave. W, Suite 360, St. Paul, MN 55114-1629
Phone: 651-647-1216　　　　Email: mail@mapnp.org
Fax: 651-647-1369　　　　　Website: www.mapnp.org

Services: MAP provides management consulting, legal counsel, financial advice, and board recruitment services to more than 500 nonprofit organizations each year.

Education: Courses and workshops are offered on leadership, computers, web design, business development, coaching, board development, financial management, and marketing.

Fees: Sliding fee scale based on the nonprofit's operating budget.

For All Artists – General Arts Organizations and Resources

Midwest Art Fairs Directory
PO Box 72, Pepin, WI 54759
Phone: 612-871-0813   Email: newnorth@cannon.net
Fax: 715-442-3027
Toll-Free: 800-871-0813

Services: *The Midwest Art Fairs Directory* includes extensive listings of all art fairs and festivals in Minnesota, Wisconsin, Iowa, North and South Dakota. Also included are special events, a variety of organization-listings, businesses, performing artists, and art studios.
Fees: Subscription is $13.95/year for the bi-annual publication.

No Name Exhibitions
PO Box 581696, Minneapolis, MN 55458-1696
Phone: 612-623-9176   Email: noname@mtn.org
                             Website: www.soapfactory.org

Services: No Name Exhibitions is a nonprofit organization dedicated to supporting emerging artists, enhancing public understanding and appreciation of their artistic expressions, and fostering strength and vitality within the artistic, cultural, and educational communities.

St. Paul Art Collective
308 Prince St., Suite 270, St. Paul, MN 55101-1437
Phone: 651-292-4373   Email: artcrawl@stpaul-artcrawl.org
                             Website: www.artcrawl.org

Services: The Saint Paul Art Collective sponsors the Saint Paul Art Crawl – a self-guided, semi-annual tour of over 170 artists' studios and galleries in the Lowertown neighborhood.

St. Paul Arts Partnership
Fax: 651-292-3391   Website: www.nowshowing.org

Services: The Saint Paul Arts Partnership works to create new opportunities for the arts in downtown Saint Paul, develop shared resources for local arts organizations, and bring audiences together to experience the arts.

For All Artists – General Arts Resources

Space: A Basic Guide to Performance and Rehearsal Spaces in Minnesota

RCA, 308 Prince St., Suite 270, St. Paul, MN 55101

Phone: 651-292-4381   Email: info@rc4arts.org
Fax: 651-292-4315   Website: www.rc4arts.org
TTY: 651-292-3218

Services: This publication is a tool for performing artists to use in finding space to practice and produce their work. Produced jointly by RCA and the Minnesota State Arts Board.

Fees: Copies free at RCA or Minnesota State Arts Board. Downloadable version available at MSAB website (www.arts.state.mn.us).

The Twin Cities Women's Art Show Collective

University YW, 244 Coffman Union
300 Washington Ave., Minneapolis, MN 55455
Phone: 612-625-0607
Fax: 612-625-9161

Services: The University YW is a student run women's social change organization which focuses on providing educational programming on issues of racism, sexism, heterosexism, and interrelated forms of inequality. They offer artists' workshops and sponsor art exhibitions through the Art Show Collaborative.

Arts Associations

American Association of Museums/ *Aviso*
1575 Eye Street NW, Suite 400, Washington, DC 20005
Phone: 202-289-9122   Email: aviso@aam-us.org
Fax: 202-789-1355   Website: www.aam-us.org/aviso/

Services: *Aviso* is the American Association of Museums' monthly newsletter providing up-to-date information about the museum field, listings on employment ads, goods, and services for museum professionals.

Fees: See website or contact AAM's Membership Department (202-289-1818) for subscription information.

Arts and Business Council Inc.
121 27th St. W, Suite 702, New York, NY 10001-6207
Phone: 212-727-7146   Email: info@artsandbusiness.org
Fax: 212-727-3873   Website: www.artsandbusiness.org

Services: Arts & Business Council Inc. is a leading national organization working to "keep the arts in business" by promoting mutually beneficial partnerships between corporations and nonprofit arts groups. Through its local and national programs the Council brings expertise, resources, and leadership talent from the business world to the arts community.

Education: Lectures, marketing project initiatives, annual award ceremonies.

Fees: $50/individual, $100/nonprofit, $500/corporate annual membership.

Minnesota Art Therapy Association
294 Janice Ave., St. Paul, MN 55126

Services: The Art Therapy Association conducts meetings three times a year. Each gathering involves discussions on business-related matters, diverse programs on art therapy, and a chance for members to network. They also publish a quarterly newsletter.

Fees: $15/student, $25/professional annual membership.

For All Artists – Arts Associations

Minnesota Artist Association
4643 18th Ave. S, Minneapolis, MN 55407
Phone: 612-722-8416 (President) Email: alsyl@earthlink.net
612-933-4807 (Membership) Website: Frogdome.com/MAA

Services: The Association is a group composed primarily of painters and sculptors who meet regularly and hold juried art exhibits at least twice a year. They have a monthly newsletter which includes news, opportunities, and announcements.

Education: Lectures, demonstrations, life drawing studio opportunities.

Fees: $20 annual membership.

National Association of Artist's Organizations (NAAO)
718 "M" Street NW, PMB #239, Washington, DC 20036
Phone: 202-347-6350 Email: naao2@artswire.org
Fax: 202-319-1107 Website: www.naao.org

Services: NAAO was established to provide its constituents with a vehicle for communication and a clear and distinct national voice. It offers services to the primary creators of new, emerging, and often experimental work. NAAO represents all disciplines, including visual, performing, media, literary, and interdisciplinary arts organizations.

National Association for the Self-Employed
PO Box 612067, DFW Airport, Dallas, TX 75261-2067
Toll-Free: 800-232-6273 Website: www.nase.org

Services: The NASE is an advocacy group for the self-employed, providing personal, business, and health benefits to its members.

Fees: Vary by level of membership.

For All Artists – Arts Associations

The National Association of Women Artists, Inc.
41 Union Square W, #906, New York, NY 10003-3278

Services: The National Association of Women Artists, Inc. (NAWA) is a nonprofit, non-political organization of women in the fine arts, whose primary purpose is to encourage and promote the creative output of women artists. NAWA seeks exhibition opportunities for its members, produces guides and publications, provides year-round juried exhibitions, and supports traveling exhibitions hosted by art centers, museums, universities, and corporate galleries.

Fees: Vary by level of membership.

Northeast Minneapolis Arts Association
2503 Central Ave. NE, #185, Minneapolis, MN 55418

Phone: 612-379-2255 ext. 12   Email: dlwood@goldengate.net

Fax: 612-379-8330   Website: www.art-a-whirl.org

Services: The NEMAA mission is to promote the quality and diversity of artistic resources in Northeast Minneapolis to benefit the greater community. The Association sponsors Art-a-Whirl, a program to open up artist studios and current work to the public on a regular basis.

The Upper Midwest Conservation Association
2400 Third Ave. S, Minneapolis, MN 55404

Phone: 612-870-3120   Email: UMCA@aol.com

Fax: 612-870-3118   Website: www.preserveart.org

Services: The Conservation Association is a nonprofit regional center for preservation and conservation of art and artifacts in the Upper Midwest region, located within the Minneapolis Institute of Art.

Education: Annual workshops are held on various art conservation topics.

For All Artists – Arts Associations/Art Councils

Women's Art Registry of Minnesota (WARM)
550 Rice St., St. Paul, MN 55103
Phone: 651-292-1188   Email: warm@rconnect.com
                              Website: www.warm.org

Services: WARM's mission is to nurture and empower women through the visual arts. The membership program for women artists includes an annual juried exhibit and bimonthly newsletters. Its mentor program pairs developing women artists with professionals. *ArtsAlive!* workshops offer continuing education for art teachers and others in Greater Minnesota. Its *Fresh Art* open monthly meetings include an opportunity for participants to get feedback on their work.

Fees: $35 annual membership. Please inquire about fees for other services.

Art Councils

East Side Arts Council
1000 Payne Ave., Second Fl., St. Paul, MN 55101
Phone: 651-774-5422   Email: esac@wavetech.net
Fax: 651-774-5502

Services: The Council provides diverse community-based arts and cultural experiences for families and individuals. They work with East Side schools, community centers, and recreation centers to carry out their mission.

Elk River Area Arts Council
400 Jackson Ave., Suite 205, Elk River, MN 55330
Phone: 763-441-4725   Email: marlys@elkriverartscouncil.com
                              Website: www.elkriverartscouncil.com

Services: The Elk River Area Arts Council is a nonprofit organization dedicated to strengthening the arts in the community by aiding and drawing attention to the activities of other arts organizations as well as through its own programs. The Arts Council serves artists and residents throughout the surrounding area including Big Lake, Nowthen, Otsego, Princeton, Ramsey, Rogers, and Zimmerman as well as drawing membership from the Twin Cities and St. Cloud areas.

Minnesota State Arts Board

Park Square Court, 400 Sibley St., Suite 200, St. Paul, MN 55101-1928
Phone: 651-215-1600   Email: msab@state.mn.us
Fax: 651-215-1602   Website: www.arts.state.mn.us
Toll-Free: 800-8MN-ARTS
TTY: 651-215-6235

Services: Offers grants, services and resource publications to individual artists, organizations, and schools throughout the state. The Board has an Arts in Education program which funds artists and arts organization residencies in K-12 schools and produces the Arts in Education Roster of Artists, a juried listing of artists available to teach in elementary and secondary schools.

Regional Arts Councils

Northwest Regional Arts Council (Region 1)

115 Main St. S, Suite 1, Warren, MN 56762
Phone: 218-745-6733   Email: mara@nwrdc.org
Fax: 218-745-6438   Website: www.nwrdc.org/arts.htm
Toll-Free: 800-646-2240

Counties: Kittson, Marshall, Norman, Pennington, Polk, Red Lake, Roseau

Services: Provides support for the development of the arts in the seven-county region through grant programs for individual artists, schools, and nonprofit organizations. A newsletter is published bimonthly. Publishes annual directory of artists, arts organizations, schools, and libraries.

Education: Workshops on grant writing are held on a request basis throughout the year.

Fees: None.

For All Artists – Art Councils

Region 2 Arts Council

426 Bemidji Ave., Bemidji, MN 56601
Phone: 218-751-5447   Email: r2arts@northnnet.com
Fax: 218-751-2777   Website: www.northernnet.com/region2arts
Toll-Free: 800-275-5447
Counties: Beltrami, Clearwater, Hubbard, Lake of the Woods, Mahnomen
Services: Promotes and funds arts creation, appreciation, and education among the people the region.

Arrowhead Regional Arts Council (Region 3)

Carnegie Building, 101 Second St. W, Suite 204, Duluth, MN 55802
Phone: 218-722-0952   Email: ARACouncil@aol.com
Fax: 218-722-4459   Website: members.aol.com/ARACouncil
Toll-Free: 800-569-8134
TTY: 800-627-3529
Counties: Aitkin, Carlton, Cook, Itasca, Koochiching, Lake, St. Louis
Services: Awards nine fellowships of $4500 each and two emerging artist fellowships of $2500 each annually to artists residing in the Arrowhead Region. Career Development Grants of up to $1000 to artists residing in the Arrowhead Region. The Fellowship Program has one deadline per year. Fees: None.

Lake Region Arts Council (Region 4)

133 Mill St. S, Fergus Falls, MN 56537
Phone: 218-739-5780   Email: Lrac@prairietech.net
Fax: 218-739-0296   Website: www.prtelweb.com/arts
Toll-Free: 800-262-ARTS (262-2787)
Counties: Becker, Clay, Douglas, Grant, Otter Tail, Pope, Stevens, Traverse, Wilkin
Services: Serves arts organizations, artists, and arts consumers through grants, technical assistance, and networking services. Their mission is to encourage and support the vitality of the arts in the nine counties of west central Minnesota.

Lake Region Arts Council, cont.

Education: The Council provides grants for school residencies and has an Artist Mentor program whereby 9th – 11th grade students can study for six months with a professional artist.

Five Wings Arts Council (Region 5)

611 Iowa Ave., Staples, MN 56479
Phone: 218-894-3233   Email: region5@brainerd.net
Fax: 218-894-1328   Website: www.fwac.org
Counties: Cass, Crow Wing, Morrison, Todd, Wadena

Services: Provides grants and services to nonprofit organizations and individuals in the region.

Southwest Minnesota Arts & Humanities Council (Regions 6E, 6W, 8)

1501 State St., FA 221, Marshall, MN 56258
Phone: 507-537-1471   Email: smach@starpoint.net
Fax: 507-537-0040   Website: www.smahc.org
Toll-Free: 800-622-5284
Counties: Big Stone, Chippewa, Cottonwood, Jackson, Kandiyohi, Lincoln, Lac Qui Parle, Lyon, McLeod, Meeker, Murray, Nobles, Pipestone, Redwood, Renville, Rock, Swift, Yellow Medicine

Services: The Southwest Minnesota Arts and Humanities Council (SMAHC) is a nonprofit organization committed to encouraging the growth and development of the arts and humanities in southwestern Minnesota by serving as a source of funds and technical services which enable local organizations and individuals to sponsor and/or create and promote the arts and humanities in their communities.

For All Artists — Art Councils

East Central Arts Council (Region 7E)
100 Park St. S, Mora, MN 55051
Phone: 320-679-4065   Email: ecac@ncis.com
Fax: 320-679-4120
Counties: Chisago, Isanti, Kanabec, Mille Lacs, Pine

Services: Provides grants of up to $1000 for projects which advance the careers of individual artists living in the region.

The Central Minnesota Arts Board (Region 7W)
PO Box 1442, St. Cloud, MN 56302
Phone: 320-253-9517   Email: mail@cmab.org
Fax: 320-253-9688   Website: www.cmab.org
Counties: Benton, Sherburne, Stearns, Wright

Services: The Central Minnesota Arts Board works to stimulate the creation, performance, and appreciation of the arts in the indicated counties by providing grants for local arts organizations or individuals.

Prairie Lakes Regional Arts Council (Region 9)
109 State St. S, Waseca, MN 56093-2951
Phone: 507-835-8721   Email: plrac@platec.net
Fax: 507-835-8799   Website: www.platec.net/~plrac/
Toll-Free: 800-298-1254
Counties: Blue Earth, Brown, Faribault, Le Sueur, Martin, Nicollet, Sibley, Waseca, Watonwan

Services: The Prairie Lakes Regional Arts Council provides a variety of funding opportunities which will promote artistic growth opportunities, organizational development, and exposure to quality arts experiences. They produce a quarterly newsletter and sponsor an annual regional juried art show. Grants are awarded to nonprofit arts organizations, community groups, schools, and individual artists.

Southeastern Minnesota Arts Council (Region 10)

1610 14th St. NW, Suite 306, Rochester, MN 55901
Phone: 507-281-4848 Email: semac@intonet.isl.net
Fax: 507-281-8373 Website: www.semac.org
Counties: Dodge, Fillmore, Freeborn, Goodhue, Houston, Olmsted, Mower, Rice, Steele, Wabasha, Winona
Services: A nonprofit organization committed to supporting and stimulating the development and diversity of the arts in southeastern Minnesota.

Metropolitan Regional Arts Council (Region 11)

2324 University Ave. W, Suite 114, St. Paul, MN 55114
Phone: 651-645-0402 Email: mrac@mrac.org
Fax: 651-523-6382 Website: www.mrac.org
Toll-Free: 800-627-3529
Counties: Anoka, Carver, Dakota, Hennepin, Ramsey, Scott, Washington
Services: MRAC is a nonprofit organization committed to supporting and stimulating the development and diversity of the arts in the seven-county metropolitan area. The council provides arts project grants, organizational development and capital grants, funds for administrative development through classes and funds for non-arts groups to attend arts events. MRAC does not fund individual artists.

Community Art Centers

Banfill-Locke Center for the Arts

6666 River Rd. E, Fridley, MN 55432
Phone: 763-574-1850
Services: Classes are offered in many different visual art disciplines for adults and children. Member and senior shows are given.

For All Artists – Community Arts Centers

Burnsville Area Society for the Arts (BASA)
1200 Alimagnet Pkwy., Box 2, Burnsville, MN 55337
Phone: 952-431-4155, ext. 2   Email: tglenn2485@aol.com
Fax: 952-431-5460
Website: www.visi.com/~witt/basa/basa1.html
Services: BASA offers art classes for all ages.

Dakota County Center for the Arts and Humanities
c/o 1750 Kyllo Ln., Eagan, MN 55122
Phone: 651-451-6755

Services: The Dakota County Center for the Arts and Humanities (also known as "The Art House") is a community based nonprofit organization whose purpose is to develop, promot,e and encourage participation of the creative arts and humanities. Located in Patrick Eagan Park, the Art House's street address is 3981 Lexington Ave.

Education: Coursework is offered to students interested in ceramics, photography, watercolor, wood & metalworking, music, writing, and more.

Edina Art Center
4701 64th St. W, Edina, MN 55435
Phone: 952-915-6600   Education: dhedges@ci.edina.mn.us
Fax: 952-915-6601
TTY: 952-927-5461
Services: The Edina Art Center exhibits are held on a rotating basis.
Education: Membership classes are offered.

Franklin ArtWorks
1021 Franklin Ave. E, Minneapolis, MN 55404
Phone: 612-872-7494   Website: www.franklinartworks.org
Fax: 612-872-7403
Services: Franklin ArtWorks is a community art center which offers programming in the visual and performing art. A theater space is scheduled

Franklin Art Works, cont.

for completion in 2001. FAW is primarily devoted to commissioning new and experimental work by Twin Cities artists, but also presents one touring exhibition each year featuring the work of nationally known artists.

Education: FAW's arts education program will begin in summer 2000 with classes and projects that will serve neighborhood youth, ages 8-18.

Hopkins Center for the Arts

1111 Main St., Hopkins, MN 55343
Phone: 952-979-1100   Email: artscenter@hopkinsmn.com
    952-979-1111 (Ticket office)
    952-979-1128 (Gallery)
Fax: 952-979-1103

Services: Classes in art, dance, and theater are offered at the Arts Center. Concerts and visual art exhibitions are presented which feature local, regional, and national artists. Performance, meeting, and classroom space is available for rent.

John Michael Kohler Arts Center

608 New York Ave., PO Box 489, Sheboygan, WI 53082-0489
Phone: 920-458-6144   Website: www.jmkac.org
Fax: 920-458-7743

Services: The Center houses art exhibitions, visual and performing arts residencies, performing arts series, shops, and a cafe.

Education: Excursions, dance classes, and workshops for preschoolers to adults.

Fees: Free admission to galleries.

For All Artists – Community Arts Centers

MacRostie Art Center

PO Box 365, 405 First Ave. NW, Grand Rapids, MN 55744
Phone: 218-326-2697   Email: macart@uslink.net
Fax: 218-326-2697

Services: The MacRostie Art Center (MAC) is a nonprofit arts organization dedicated to the exhibition of and education in the visual arts. It features a spacious gallery with monthly rotating art exhibits, and also contains classrooms, a visual resource library, and a consignment gift shop where original artwork is available for purchase.

Education: MAC educational programming is year-round and includes classes and workshops for youth and adults in a wide variety of media.

Fees: No admission is charged for visitors. $20 annual membership.

Minneapolis American Indian Center/Two Rivers Gallery

1530 Franklin Ave. E, Minneapolis, MN55404
Phone: 612-879-1780   Email: jespinson@MAICnet.org
Fax: 612-879-1795   Website: www.nativeartscircle.org

Services: The Center and Gallery are an information resource for Native American artists. Exhibitions are held throughout the year.

Education: Lectures, educational programs, outreach activities.

Minnetonka Center for the Arts

2240 Shore Dr. N, Wayzata, MN 55391
Phone: 952-473-7361, Ext. 16   Email: mtkarts@uswest.net
Fax: 952-473-7363

Services: Studio art classes are offered in drawing, painting, sculpture, photography, pottery, and fiber arts. Regional artists are featured in two galleries; catalogs also available.

Fees: Classes are approximately $6/hr. plus lab fees.

Nobles County Art Center

407 12th St., PO Box 313, Worthington, MN 56187
Phone: 507-372-8245

Services: Features a book club, fine film series, art exhibits, and sales.

Pillsbury House

3501 Chicago Ave. S, Minneapolis, MN 55407
Phone: 612-824-0708
Fax: 612-827-5818

Services: Pillsbury House has studio facilities for music, art, dance, and theater. Their performance space is often used for small community productions.

Education: Classes in music, art, dance, and theater for children and adults.

Rochester Art Center

320 Center St. E, Rochester, MN 55904
Phone: 507-282-8629   Email: rdh@hps.com
Fax: 507-282-7737   Website: www.rochesterusa.com/artcenter

Services: Rochester Art Center is a center for the visual arts, providing art education, outreach programs, exhibitions, and special events to the region.

Education: Classes, workshops, film presentations, lectures, and gallery tours are available for all ages.

Waseca Art Center

410 State St. N, Waseca, MN 56093
Phone: 507-835-1701   Email: WAC@mnic.net
Fax: 507-835-1701

Services: The Waseca Art Center offers cultural enrichment programs including monthly art exhibitions, an art appreciation series for area school districts, and a variety of art classes for adults and children. Other Center services are a book and video library, a photography club, occasional cultural trips, and a permanent collection of art.

Education: Continuing series of education opportunities available for children and adults.

Fees: Vary.

Cultural Centers

American Indian Resource and Referral Database

Website: www.airr.net   Email: gmccauley@maicnet.org

Services: The American Indian Resource and Referral Database is an online resource designed to help Native Americans and social service workers find Native cultural and social services in the Minneapolis/St.Paul area. Currently there are over 230 organizations listed.

The American Swedish Institute

2600 Park Ave. S, Minneapolis, MN 55407

Phone: 612-871-4907   Email: information@americanswedishinst.org

Fax: 612-871-8682   Website: www.americanswedishinst.org/general.htm

Services: The American Swedish Institute is a historic house/museum offering programs designed to celebrate Swedish culture. They offer exhibits and special events relating to Swedish arts, history, and culture.

Education: Classes, workshops, and lectures offered.

Fees: Admission is $4, $3 senior citizens, $2 children 6-12 years old.

Asian American Renaissance

1564 LaFond Ave., St. Paul, MN 55104

Phone: 651-641-4040   Email: arenaissance@earthlink.net

Fax: 651-641-4041

Services: The AAR is a networking and presenting group which holds conferences, performance presentations, screenings, and exhibitions. They are also a resource for Asian American artists in all genres.

Education: Residency workshops, educational programs.

Association for the Advancement of Hmong Women in Minnesota

1518 Lake St. E, Suite 209, Minneapolis, MN 55407

Phone: 612-724-3066

Fax: 612-724-3098

For All Artists – Cultural Centers

Association for the Advancement of Hmong Women in Minnesota, cont.

Services: The Association exists to help and support Hmong women, girls and families, enrich their sense of Hmong culture and celebrate their new life in America. Offers employment services, Hmong dance, cultural classes, and outreach projects.

Cedar Cultural Center

416 Cedar Ave. S, Minneapolis, MN 55454
Phone: 612-338-2674   Email: info@thecedar.org
Fax: 612-338-1687   Website: www.thecedar.org

Services: Cedar Cultural Center supports traditional ethnic music and dance through their variety of programs and shows.

Center for Asians and Pacific Islanders

3702 Lake St. E, Minneapolis, MN 55407
Phone: 612-721-0122   Email: info@capiusa.org
Fax: 612-721-7054   Website: www.capiusa.org

Services: The Center is a direct service and informational agency that assists Southeast Asian and Pacific Islander families to contribute to the economic and social fabric of Minnesota while maintaining their unique cultural heritage and values.

Centro Cultural Chicano

2025 Nicollet Ave. S, Minneapolis, MN 55404
Phone: 612-874-1412   Email: centro@uswest.net
Fax: 612-874-8149

Services: Centro has a variety of radio programs on KFAI. Their Arts and Cultural Awareness program has events for cultural vitality and pride. Along with these arts-related programs, the Centro provides employment resources, mental health counseling, crisis intervention, an early childhood development program, a food shelf, clothes closet, and an extensive network of referrals to miscellaneous needs.

For All Artists – Cultural Centers

Chicano Latinos unidos en Servicios (CLUES)

220 Robert St. S, Suite 103, St. Paul, MN 55107
2110 Nicollet Ave. S, Minneapolis, MN 55404
Phone: 651-292-0117 (St. Paul); 612-871-0200 (Mpls)
Fax: 651-292-0347 (St. Paul); 612-871-1058 (Mpls)
Website: www.clues.org

Services: Chicanos Latinos Unidos En Servicio, Inc. (CLUES) is a private nonprofit organization that provides linguistically and culturally appropriate services to the Chicano Latino community. CLUES has developed a continuum of services within the core areas of Mental Health, Chemical Health, Employment, Education, and Seniors.

Education: The main focus of their education program is English as a Second Language (ESL) tutoring. CLUES also provides bilingual assistance and training for citizenship.

CreArte

1515 Lake St. E, Suite 210, Minneapolis, MN 55407
Phone: 612-813-1953   Email: create@mtn.org
                             Website: www.CreArte.org

Services: The purpose of CreArte is to serve as a community based arts and cultural activities resource for the Mexicano, Chicano, and Latino communities in the state of Minnesota. They provide a local artist registry, present various folk arts and Latino workshops, and sponsor the annual Dia de los Muertos celebration. An emergency fund has been set up with certain restrictions.

Instituto de Arte y Cultura

3501 Chicago Ave. S, Minneapolis, MN 55407
Phone: 612-824-0708 Ext. 16
Fax: 612-827-5818

Services: The Instituto keeps an artist roster of Hispanic Chicano and Latino/Latina performing, media, literary, and visual artists. They also provide consulting aid for all artists participating in their programs. They hold a performing arts series, storytelling workshops, and folkloric dance classes focusing on the Hispanic culture.

For All Artists – Cultural Centers

Irish Music & Dance Association

PO Box 65187, St. Paul, MN 55165

Phone: 612-721-7452   Email: mnimda@hotmail.com

Fax: 612-721-7452 (call first)

Services: The IMDA publishes a listing of local Irish musicians, dance groups, music and dance instruction; publishes a monthly cultural newsletter, and sponsors Irish music and dance events in the Twin Cities.

Education: Referrals for Irish music and dance instruction.

Fees: $15/individual, $20/family annual membership.

Jewish Community Center of Greater Minneapolis

4330 Cedar Lake Rd. S, St. Louis Park, MN 55416

Phone: 952-377-8330   Website: www.minneapolisjcc.org

Services: The JCC is a nonprofit agency which serves the social, cultural, educational, and recreational needs of more than 5000 people of all ages in the Minneapolis area. Cultural arts are emphasized as an important part of their program.

Education: Classes for adults and children are offered in many disciplines.

Fees: Membership fee depends on age, and single/family status. Financial assistance is provided to those who are unable to pay the full cost of membership.

Jewish Community Center of the Greater St. Paul Area

1375 St. Paul Ave., St. Paul, MN 55116-2798

Phone: 651-698-0751   Email: mladinov@stpauljcc.org

Fax: 651-698-8591

Services: The Center has a library, different visual arts and music studios, exhibitions, and performances.

Education: Classes are offered for adults and children in music, dance, visual arts, and writing. They hold an annual book fair which includes visiting writers, lecturers, and workshops.

For All Artists – Cultural Centers/Community Broadcast/Newspapers

Minneapolis American Indian Center/Two Rivers Gallery
See page 18.

Rimon Jewish Metropolitan Council on Arts and Culture
The Department of Identity & Continuity, Minneapolis Jewish Federation
13100 Wayzata Blvd., Suite 200, Minnetonka, MN 55305
Phone: 952-417-2353 Email: hherring@mplsfed.org
Fax: 952-593-2544

Services: The Council has established a program called Rimon, which is designed to promote and enhance Jewish identity through arts and culture.

Community Television Broadcast

Performing artists interested in creating a videotaped work sample are advised to contact their local cable provider for more information about public access studio availability. Your community broadcast television stations are listed in the phone book. Working in their studios is often an easy, inexpensive way to create a work sample for grant applications, tour promotion, and archival purposes.

Community Newspapers

Asian American Press
417 University Ave., St. Paul, MN 55103
Phone: 651-224-6570 Website: www.aapress.com

Services: The Asian American Press is a local newspaper for the Asian American community. It is published every Thursday, and distributed every Friday at over 400 locations throughout the Metro area.

For All Artists – Community Newspapers

The Circle
Minneapolis American Indian Center
1530 Franklin Ave. E, Minneapolis, MN 55404
Phone: 612-879-1760   Email: CircleMPLS@aol.com
Fax: 612-879-1712   Website: www.thecircleonline.org
Services: The Circle is dedicated to presenting reports from a Native American perspective to its readers, while granting an equal opportunity to community voices.

La Prensa de Minnesota
417 University Ave., St. Paul, MN 55103
Phone: 651-224-0404   Email: laprensa@winternet.com
Fax: 651.224.0098   Website: www.laprensa-mn.com
Services: La Prensa de Minnesota is a local newspaper for Minnesota's Hispanic community.

The Minnesota Women's Press
771 Raymond Ave., St. Paul, MN 55114
Phone: 651-646-3968   Email: women@womenspress.com
Fax: 651-646-2186   Website: www.womenspress.com
Services: The mission of Minnesota Women's Press, Inc., is to promote communication by, about, and among women in ways that create community and are grounded in a transforming feminist worldview.

Arts Education

Artward Bound/Summit Arts
St. Paul Academy, 1712 Randolph Ave., St. Paul, MN 55105
Phone: 651-696-1355   Email: mspewock@admin.spa.edu
Fax: 651-698-6787   Website: www.spa.edu

Services: Artward Bound/Summit Arts provide summer programs for children ages 4-14 who want to explore the fine and performing arts.
Education: Multi-arts classes for ages 9-14; integrated arts for ages 4-8.
Fees: Three-week sessions are $625, Six-week sessions are $1050. Individual classes can also be taken in Artward Bound. Scholarships available.

Caponi Art Park & Learning Center
1205 Diffley Rd., Eagan, MN 55123
Phone: 651-454-9412   Email: mail@caponiartpark.org
Fax: 651-454-9412   Website: www.caponiartpark.org

Services: The Art Park provides a cultural center where people of different talents and interests come together with art and nature to restore, nurture, and maintain the human spirit. Primarily an outdoor venue. Presentations include a Summer Performance Series of concerts and plays and a summer children's series called Family Fun Tuesdays.
Education: Children's art camps are held in July and August. Guided tours can be scheduled any time.

Center for Arts Criticism
2822 Lyndale Ave. S, Minneapolis, MN 55408
Phone: 612-874-2818
Fax: 612-871-6927

Services: The Center was created for the sole purpose of addressing the need for more quantity, quality, and diversity in arts and cultural criticism. It works in partnership with critics, artists, youth, and arts organizations to increase the understanding of how the arts are connected to everyday life.

College of Visual Arts

344 Summit Ave., St. Paul, MN 55102
Phone: 651-224-3416   Website: www.cva.edu
Fax: 651-224-8854

Services: The College of Visual Arts is a private, four-year college of art and design, located in the Summit Hill area of Saint Paul. The College offers Bachelor of Fine Arts degrees in Visual Communications (communication design, illustration, photography) and Fine Arts (painting, drawing, sculpture, printmaking, general fine arts).

COMPAS

See page 3.

JuxtaPosition Arts

See page 4.

MacPhail Center for the Arts

See page 56.

Minneapolis College of Art & Design

2501 Stevens Ave. S, Minneapolis, MN 55404
Phone: 612-874-3760   Email: admissions@mn.mcad.edu
Fax: 612-874-3704   Website: www.mcad.edu
Toll-Free: 800-874-6223 TTY: 612-874-3800

Services: MCAD offers superb prospects for careers in the arts. Students can choose among four programs: Bachelor of Science: Visualization, Bachelor of Fine Arts in 14 majors, Post Baccalaureate Certificate, and a Master of Fine Arts in Visual Studies.

Education: Day and extension program classes for graduate and undergraduate students.

Fees: Tuition and studio access fees vary.

For All Artists – Arts Education

Minnesota Alliance for Arts in Education

2233 University Avenue W, Suite 233, St. Paul, MN 55114

Phone: 651-917-9000   Email: info@allarts4allkids.org
Fax: 651-917-8000   Website: www.allarts4allkids.org
Toll-Free: 800-833-6223

Services: The Alliance strives as a grassroots advocacy organization to ensure high quality learning in music, visual arts, dance, theater, literary arts, and media arts as an essential part of the K-12 education of every Minnesota child.

Minnesota River School of Fine Art

190 River Ridge Cir. S, Burnsville, MN 55337

Phone: 952-890-4182   Email: info@mrsfa.com
Fax: 952-890-0231   Website: www.mrsfa.com

Services: The Minnesota River School offers artistic course studies for full and part-time students covering a broad range of disciplines in a variety of media. Exhibitions, workshops, seminars, and conferences for visiting artists are also presented at the school.

Minnesota State Arts Board

See page 11.

National Art Education Association

1916 Association Dr., Reston, VA 20191-1590

Phone: 703-860-8000   Email: naea@dgs.dgsys.com
Fax: 703-860-2960   Website: www.naea-reston.org

Services: National Art Education Association's purpose is to promote art education through professional development, service, advancement of knowledge, and leadership. The Association publishes books, journals, reports, surveys, flyers, and other materials which further their cause.

Fees: Vary by level of membership.

For All Artists – Arts Education

Origins Program

4632 Vincent Ave. S, Minneapolis, MN 55410

Phone: 612-822-3422 Website: www.originsonline@mtn.org

Services: The Origins Program plans residencies and educational programs in elementary and secondary schools and has a focus on multi- and cross-cultural issues. They have an artists' roster from which they draw.

The Studio

B-70 Coffman Union, 300 Washington Ave. SE, Minneapolis, MN 55455

Phone: 612-625-9918 Website: www.coffman.umn.edu/underground/studio

Fax: 612-626-2966

Services: Mini-Courses and Workshops at The Studio provide University of Minnesota students and other members of the campus and local communities the opportunity to develop and refine skills in the visual arts while meeting other people doing the same.

Education: Assorted classes in watercolor, calligraphy, drawing, and more.

West Bank School of Music

1813 Sixth St. S, Minneapolis, MN 55454

Phone: 612-333-6651 Email: eesse@mtn.org

Toll-Free: 800-224-1536 Website: www.westbankmusic.org

Services: West Bank School of Music offers private and group instruction in folk, rock, jazz, blues, country, bluegrass, pop, and classical music.

Education: Classes and lessons.

Fees: For class and registration, contact admissions office toll-free number.

Young Audiences of Minnesota

416 Landmark Center, 75 Fifth St. W, St. Paul, MN 55102-1414

Phone: 651-292-3399 Email: yamn@bitstream.net

Fax: 651-292-3397 Website: www.yamn.org

Services: Young Audiences of Minnesota is the local chapter of Young Audiences, Inc., a national advocate for arts-in-education services. They bring performances, workshops, residencies, art exhibitions, master classes,

For All Artists – Arts Education/Public Art

Young Audiences of Minnesota, cont.

and professional development for educators to schools and other community settings – all by acclaimed, professional local artists. They provide roster artists with a statewide network of schools and community organizations seeking arts education programs, and administrative/contractual support. Annual auditions are held for artists interested in being on the roster.
Fees: Vary.

Public Art

FORECAST Public Artworks

2324 University Ave. W, Suite 102, St. Paul, MN 55114
Phone: 651-641-1028   Email: forecast@mtn.org
Fax: 612-644-3642   Website: www.forecast.org

Services: FORECAST Public Artworks supports the development and appreciation of public art by creating opportunities for artists and communities to explore the public realm. FORECAST also offers expertise to artists, organizations, and agencies interested in incorporating public art into their communities through the public art services program.

Office of Cultural Affairs: Minneapolis Arts Commission

350 Fifth St. S, City Hall Room 302, Minneapolis, MN 55415-3029
Phone: 612-673-3006   Website: www.ci.minneapolis.mn.us
Fax: 612-673-2933
Email: Stephanie.Krusemark@ci.minneapolis.mn.us
TTY: 612-673-2157

Services: The Commission works with the arts community and neighborhood community organizations to develop programs and policies which benefit the arts and the city. Their programs are: Art in Public Places, Neighborhood Arts Program, and Art in the Mayor's Office Program.

Public Art St. Paul

Minnesota Building, Suite 828, 46 Fourth St. E, St. Paul, MN 55105
Phone: 651-290-0921   Email: cpl@gcl.com
Fax: 651-222-2141

Services: This organization administers most public art projects – city, county, and those privately sponsored – that are planned for the St. Paul area. Commissions are chosen through calls for artists and a slide registry.

Helpful Websites

ArtNetwork: www.artmarketing.com

Services: ArtNetwork is a publisher of art marketing books and newsletters, as well as other resources for fine artists. ArtNetwork teaches artists to market and sell art work, connecting them to art world professionals, consultants, galleries, etc., to advance their careers.

Arts and Business Council Inc.: www.artsandbusiness.org

See page 7.

ArtSource: www.ilpi.com/Artsource/artsourcehome.html

Services: ArtSource is a gathering point for networked resources on Art and Architecture. Content includes pointers to resources around the net as well as original materials submitted by librarians, artists, art historians, etc.

Internet ArtResources: www.artresources.com

Services: Internet ArtResources provides listings of galleries, artists, museums, schools and shows, and updates its roster daily. Articles, reviews, and news items are also added to the website each week.

Information by Art Form

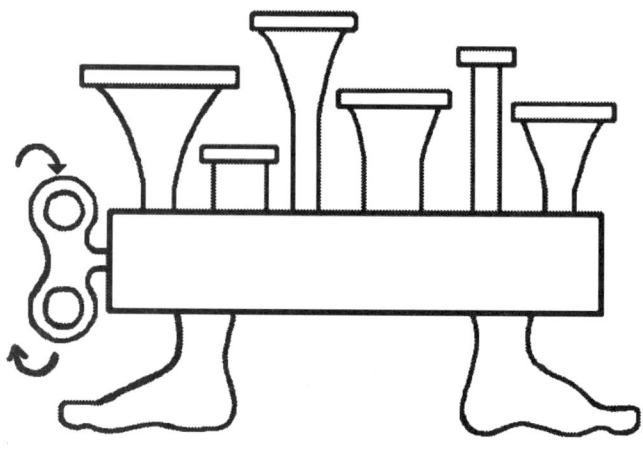

Resources for Visual Artists	33
Watercolor	35
Cartooning	36
Sculpture	37
Wood & Metal	38
Design	40
Film & Video	43
Photography	45
Website Construction	47
Crafts	48
Ceramics	49
Fiber Arts & Textiles	50
Music	55
Theater & Performance	61
Dance	63
Storytelling	65
Writing & Literature	66
Book & Paper Arts	69

Resources for Visual Artists

Art Calendar Magazine
PO Box 199, Upper Fairmount, MD 21867
Phone: 410-651-0443   Website: www.artcalendar.com

Services: *Art Calendar Magazine* is published 11 times a year with each issue containing 40-56 pages. It includes information on national art markets, job listings, and current art trends.

Fees: $32 annual subscription.

Artists Del Norte
PO Box 312, Anoka, MN 55303

Services: Meetings for Artists Del Norte are held monthly at the Riverwind Recreation Center. The organization sponsors juried shows, guest speakers, workshops, gallery tours, and a monthly newsletter.

Art Scraps
1459 St. Clair Ave., St. Paul, MN 55105
Phone: 651-698-2787

Services: Art Scraps is a creative materials re-use store that provides low-cost materials and programming for individuals, groups, and communities. Discards and scrap materials are donated by local companies, families, artists, or educators, and community groups buy the inexpensive materials for artistic and educational purposes.

Ax-man Surplus
1639 University Ave. W, St. Paul, MN 55104
Phone: 651-646-8653

Services: Ax-man Surplus sells art scraps, materials, and industrial supplies. Ax-man stores also located in St. Louis Park, Bloomington, and Fridley.

Info by Art Form – Resources for Visual Artists

Exhibit: A Basic Guide to Gallery and Exhibition Spaces in Minnesota

RCA, 308 Prince St., Suite 270, St. Paul, MN 55101
Phone: 651-292-4381 Email: info@rc4arts.org
Fax: 651-292-4315 Website: www.rc4arts.org
TTY: 651-292-3218

Services: *Exhibit* is intended for visual artists wishing to locate new venues to exhibit and sell their work, and for art patrons and collectors. Includes listings of commercial and alternative galleries, museums, and nonprofit galleries, as well as tips for marketing artwork and dealing with galleries. Fees: Copies free at RCA or Minnesota State Arts Board. Downloadable version available at MSAB website (www.arts.state.mn.us).

Minnesota Artist Association

See page 7.

Minnesota Artists Exhibition Program

c/o Minneapolis Institute of Arts, 2400 Third Ave. S, Minneapolis, MN 55404
Phone: 612-870-3125 Fax: 612-870-3004

Services: MAEP presents an ongoing schedule of exhibitions by Minnesota Artists. There are five exhibitions per year and the selection process is ongoing. Panel selected to review slides are elected by the community at an annual meeting. They meet monthly to review slides artists have submitted.

The ReUse Center

Hi-Lake Shopping Center, 2216 Lake St. E, Minneapolis, MN 55407
Phone: 612-724-2608 Email: jwisdom@reusecenter.org
Fax: 612-724-2288

Services: The ReUse Center harvests material from the waste stream and sells it to provide jobs for area residents. Artists can donate or find reusable building materials at The Center.

The Studio

See page 29.

Info by Art Form —Resources for Visual Artists/Watercolor

Visual Artist Information Hotline

New York Foundation for the Arts
155 Avenue of the Americas, New York, NY 10013-1507
Toll-Free: 800-232-2789   Email: hotline@nyfa.org
Fax: 212-366-1778   Website: www.nyfa.org/vaih

Services: The Visual Artist Information Hotline is a free information service for individual artists working in all visual arts media (painting, sculpture, photography, film, video, drawing, printmaking, performance art, crafts, etc). The Hotline empowers visual artists by providing them with complete information about resources to facilitate their work.
Fees: None.

Women in Photography and Visual Arts

1255 Ashland Ave., Suite 1, St. Paul, MN 55104
Phone: 612-729-2079

Services: This group is a network/resource for commercial and fine arts photographers, graphic artists, and visual artists. They publish a quarterly newsletter, present exhibitions during the year, and hold monthly meetings with speakers, workshops, and networking.
Fees: $30 annual membership.

Watercolor

Lake Country Pastel Society

728 Torchwood Dr., New Brighton, MN 55112
Phone: 651-636-1427   Email: bjornson@usinternet.com

Services: Lake Country Pastel Society seeks to unite artists interested in the pastel medium and serve their needs by encouraging artistic growth, development through education, sharing ideas, and by creating public awareness of pastel as a unique and beautiful art form.
Education: Workshops, demonstrations, meetings, and exhibits.
Fees: $25 annual membership.

Info by Art Form – Watercolor/Cartooning

Minnesota Watercolor Society

4011 Chicago Ave. S, Minneapolis, MN 55407
Phone: 612-824-6460   Email: mardi4011@aol.com
Services: The Society holds monthly meetings, bi-annual exhibitions, summer paint-outs, and also publishes a monthly newsletter, *Brushstrokes*.
Education: Workshops, demonstrations, and lectures.
Fees: $25/individual, $35/family annual membership.

Northstar Watercolor Society

4399 Snail Lake Court W, Shoreview, MN 55126
Phone: 651-484-5026
Services: The Society holds monthly meetings during the school year, paint-outs in the summer, workshops, and one annual exhibition.

Cartooning

Cartoon Connections

PO Box 10899, White Bear Lake, MN 55110
Phone: 651-426-5278   Email: cartoonc@aol.com
                             Website: www.cartoonconnections.com
Services: Cartoon Connections is affiliated with the Minnesota State Arts Board. Duane and Angie Barnhart teach cartooning, and offer tips on creating characters.
Education: Classes through various organizations.

Minnesota Cartoonists League

3112 Holmes Ave. S, Minneapolis, MN 55408
Phone: 612-825-2653
Services: The Minnesota Cartoonists League is an informal networking group for cartoon artists with monthly meetings which include speakers on business and artistic issues. They also refer artists to clients and publish a quarterly newsletter.
Fees: No membership fee.

Sculpture

Franconia Sculpture Park

29815 Unity Ave., Shafer, MN 55074

Phone: 651-465-3701 (Director)   Website: www.franconia.org

Fax: 651-465-3701

Services: Franconia Sculpture Park supports emerging artists and mature sculptors from Minnesota and around the world in an outdoor environment. They offer ten FSP/Jerome Foundation fellowships per year; proposals are due at the end of February each year.

Education: Sculpture symposiums, sculpting for kids, and weekly tours.

Fees: Donations are accepted.

International Sculpture Center

14 Fairgrounds Rd., Suite B, Hamilton, NJ 08619-3447

Phone: 609-689-1051   Email: isc@sculpture.org

Fax: 609-689-1061   Website: www.sculpture.org

Services: The ISC advances the creation and understanding of sculpture through international conferences, *Sculpture Magazine*, an on-line slide registry and referral system, and special events. Membership is open to sculptors and those interested in sculpture. The Center offers group health and fine art insurance, including artwork (raw materials, works-in progress, finished work), studio equipment, and work-in-transit.

National Sculpture Society

At America's Tower, 1117 Avenue of the Americas, New York, NY 10036

Phone: 212-764-5645   Email: info@nationalsculpture.org

Fax: 212-764-5651   Website: www.nationalsculpture.org

Services: The National Sculpture Society is the oldest organization of professional sculptors in the United States. They offer grants, scholarships, annual awards, and a quarterly publication, *Sculpture Review*. Members are eligible for discounted health, dental, and disability insurance.

Fees: Vary by level of membership.

Info by Art Form – Sculpture/Wood & Metal

Sculptor.Org

Email: sculptor@sculptor.org   Website: www.Sculptor.Org

Services: Sculptor.Org is a comprehensive online resource guide for sculptors and those interested in the art of sculpture. This site is used to advertise for a sculptor, find out information about a particular sculpture, locate reference books on sculpting, and look for job openings in the field.
Fees: None.

Wood & Metal

Guild of Metalsmiths

PO Box 11423, St. Paul, MN 55111
Fax: 612-441-5846   Email: gene@mtn.org
Website: www.metalsmith.org

Services: The Guild is a network of approximately 350 metalsmiths located mostly in the Upper Midwest, whose emphasis is on blacksmithing, metalsmithing of all types, and jewelry making. They hold bimonthly meetings, have a videotape library, and publish a quarterly magazine.
Education: Frequent workshops (about 30 a year), annual spring and fall conferences.
Fees: $30 annual membership, conference fees are about $35, workshop fees vary from $10 - $180 depending on duration and materials.

Minnesota Wood Carvers' Association

3212 88th St. W, Bloomington, MN 55431
Phone: 952-831-4276

Services: The MN Wood Carvers' Association holds monthly meetings with demonstrations and lectures, has a yearly exhibition, and publishes a monthly newsletter. Chapter clubs are developing throughout the state, making the Bloomington location the parent organization.
Fees: $15 annual membership.

Minnesota Woodturners Association

558 Farrell St., Maplewood, MN 55119
Phone: 651-484-9094

Services: The Woodturners Association's monthly meetings usually center on demonstrations by members of various skill levels in addition to providing a venue for members to learn from each other and share in their own skills. Their newsletter includes technical information, a summary of past meetings, and schedules of upcoming meetings and events.

Education: Annual all-day workshop.

Fees: $15 annual membership.

Minnesota Woodworkers Guild

4728 Abbott Ave. S, Minneapolis, MN 55410
Phone: 612-544-7278   Email: rgotz@empros.com
                             Website: www.visi.com/~jzinsli

Services: The Minnesota Woodworkers Guild is a group of professional and amateur woodworkers, bound together to educate themselves and the public about woodworking, and to advocate high standards in the craft. The Guild holds exhibitions, monthly meetings, and publishes a newsletter.

Fees: $30 annual membership.

The Wood Carving Store and School

3056 Excelsior Blvd., Minneapolis, MN 55416
Phone: 612-927-7491
Fax: 612-927-0324

Services: The Wood Carving Store sells tools of the trade, while the School offers classes in the art of woodcarving.

Education: Classes offered in woodcarving.

Info by Art Form – Wood & Metal/Design

The Wooden Cove
1472 Yankee Doodle Rd., Eagan, MN 55122
Phone: 651-456-9475

Services: Offers classes using woods and acrylics. Classes are available in calligraphy, folk art, rosemaling, and woodcarving.
Fees: Vary per class.

Design

American Institute of Architects
275 Market St., Suite 54, Minneapolis, MN 55405-1621
Phone: 612-338-6763   Email: hauschild@aia-mn.org
Fax: 612-338-7981   Website: www.e-architect.com

Services: Provides easy access for architects to all their building needs. It is also a resource for professional architects to find work.

American Institute of Graphic Arts
164 Fifth Ave., New York, NY 10010
Phone: 212-807-1990   Email: AIGAnswers@aiga.org
Fax: 212-807-1799   Website: www.aiga.org

Services: The AIGA is a national organization committed to the promotion of excellence in graphic design. AIGA members are eligible to apply for medical insurance plans in most states.

American Institute of Graphic Arts, Minnesota Chapter
275 Market St., Suite 54, Minneapolis, MN 55405
Phone: 612-339-6904   Email: AIBAmn@aol.com
Toll-Free: 800-548-1634 Website: www.aiga.org

Services: Provides news and resources for emerging and established designers. Group health insurance is available to members.
Fees: $45/student, $75/professional group, $170/associate membership.

Info by Art Form – Design

American Society of Interior Designers, Minneapolis Chapter
275 Market St., Suite C27, Minneapolis, MN 55405
Phone: 612-339-6003   Email: asid@asid.org
         202-546-3480 (National)   Website: www.asid.org
Fax: 612-339-8691
         202-546-3240 (National)

Services: ASID establishes a common identity for professionals and businesses in the field of interior design. ASID is a resource for professional education and knowledge, sharing, advocacy of interior designers' right to practice, and expansion of interior design markets.

Fees: Vary by level of membership.

Children's Book Illustrators Guild
Phone: 651-224-0544 (membership)
Email: skylarker@earthling.net   Website: www.childrens-illustrators.net

Services: The Guild is a resource and support group for artists working in the children's book illustration and literature field. Monthly meetings at homes of members include information sharing, portfolio reviews, demonstrations, guest lecturers, and field trips. It publishes a newsletter.

Freelancers Group
1310 Spruce Pl., Mound, MN 55369
Phone: 952-471-7171   Email: fcnet@uswest.net
Fax: 952-471-7903

Services: This group meets monthly to discuss and receive expert advice on issues dealing with the communications industry. Members include editors, writers, graphic designers, illustrators, photographers, and persons in public relations and marketing. A monthly newspaper is distributed.

Education: Lectures and short workshops.

Info by Art Form – Design

Graphic Artists Guild

90 John St., Suite 403, New York, NY 10038-3202
Phone: 212-791-3400   Email: pr@gag.org
Fax: 212-791-0333   Website: www.gag.org
Toll-Free: 800-500-2672

Services: The Graphic Artists Guild is a national union committed to promoting and protecting the economic interests of its members, improving conditions for graphic artists, and raising standards for the entire industry. Membership benefits include educational programs, job hotlines, discounts on products and services, a legal referral network, grievance handling, contract consultation, and Guild publications.

Minnesota Society of Children's Book Writers and Illustrators

PO Box 46163, Plymouth, MN 55446-0163
Phone: 763-416-5385   Email: vicki@isd.net
                           Website: www.minnskibwee.com

Services: The Minnesota chapter of SCBWI hosts spring and fall conferences, several workshops, and provides networking and resources for writers and illustrators.

Education: A Nuts 'n' Bolts Workshop provides answers to beginning writers' and illustrators' frequently asked questions.

Fees: Annual membership dues.

Siggraph

16650 Marystown Rd., Shakopee, MN 55379
Phone: 612-721-6642

Services: This group meets monthly to discuss and network about computer graphics, design, and animation. A newsletter is also produced.

Film & Video

Academy for Film and Television

6651 Hwy. 7, St. Louis Park, MN 55426

Phone: 952-915-9132 Website: www.caryninternational.com

Fax: 952-915-9181

Services: The Academy was set up to be a conservatory-level training school for actors in the Twin Cities. They are particularly equipped to accommodate those actors who seek on-camera experience to compete in the commercial, industrial, and film markets.

Education: Classes for beginning to advanced students, ages seven to adult.

Association of Independent Video and Filmmakers (AIVF)

304 Hudson St., Sixth Fl., New York, NY 10013

Phone: 212-807-1400 Email: info@aivf.org

Fax: 212-463-8519 Website: www.aivf.org

Services: The Association of Independent Video and Filmmakers (AIVF) is a national membership organization serving international filmmakers and videomakers. Their services and resources include: informative seminars and networking events; trade discounts and access to group health and production insurance; advocacy for media arts issues; a public resource library; and publication of books and directories. *The Independent Film & Video Monthly* magazine is dedicated to the diverse issues facing the independent media field.

Fees: $55/Individual, $35/Student, $95/Dual, $150/Business-Industry, $100/Nonprofit annual membership.

Independent Feature Project/North

401 Third St. N, Suite 450, Minneapolis, MN 55401

Phone: 612-338-0871 Email: word@ifpnorth.org

Fax: 612-338-4747 Website: www.ifp.org

Services: IFP/North is a nonprofit arts organization whose mission is to encourage the quality and diversity of independent film production.

Fees: $55/student, $85/individual, $150/household annual membership.

Info by Art Form – Film & Video

International Documentary Association
1551 Robertson Blvd. S, Suite 201, Los Angeles, CA 90035-4257
Phone: 310-284-8422   Email: ida@artnet.net
Fax: 310-785-9334   Website: www.documentary.org

Services: The IDA is a nonprofit association, founded in 1982 to raise public consciousness of the documentary's importance. Health insurance plans are made available to members and are specifically intended for film and video artists.

Fees: $35/student, $50/individual annual membership.

Midwest Media Artists Access Center
2388 University Ave. W, 2nd fl., St. Paul, MN 55114
Phone: 651-644-1912   Email: mmaac@mtn.org
Fax: 651-644-5708   Website: www.mtn.org/mmaac

Services: MMAAC provides media artists with low-cost access to film and photo equipment and facilities, offers media arts classes, hosts member film screenings and photo exhibits, and sponsors the "Works" media access grant program.

Education: Classes in film, photography, digital filmmaking, and specialty workshops are offered year round. Registration procedures for workshops and special events are announced through the quarterly newsletter and posted online.

Fees: $35-$95 by level of annual membership.

Minneapolis Office of Cultural Affairs – Film, Video, Recording & New Media
302 City Hall, 350 Fifth St. S, Minneapolis, MN, 55415-1300
Phone: 612-673-2947   Email: Nicole.Hinrichs-Bideau@ci.minneapolis.mn.us
Fax: 612-673-2933   Website: www.ci.minneapolis.mn.us/arts

Services: The Office works to connect people interested in the fields of film, video, recording, and new media to Minnesota industry professionals. They publish *Mastering Media in Minnesota*, a guide to education resources in the area.

Info by Art Form – Film & Video/Photography

Minnesota Film Board

401 Third St. N, Suite 460, Minneapolis, MN 55401
Phone: 612-332-6493   Email: info@mnfilm.org
Fax: 612-332-3735   Website: www.mnfilm.org

Services: The primary purpose of the Film Board is to promote Minnesota as a viable production site for film and video. They publish a book, *Minnesota Production Guide*, which lists local film and video freelancers in all related jobs and fields. Paid and unpaid internships available.

University Film Society

2331 University Ave. SE, Suite 130 B, Minneapolis, MN 55414
Phone: 612-627-4431   Email: filmsoc@tc.umn.edu
Fax: 612-627-4111   Website: www.ufilm.org

Services: The University Film Society exhibits cinema, mostly American independent and foreign films, and hosts the Minneapolis/St Paul International Film Festival (formerly Rivertown) every year. Programs are presented at Bell Museum Auditorium at the University of Minnesota.

Photography

American Society of Media Photographers, Minneapolis/St Paul Chapter

4125 Chowen Ave. S, Minneapolis, MN 55410
Phone: 612-929-6010   Email: info@asmp-msp.org
Fax: 612-929-4230   Website: www.asmp-msp.org

Services: The Society is an advocacy group, and does legal referrals as well. Members of the Society are eligible for life, comprehensive medical, major medical, disability, and camera insurance. Additional coverage may be obtained for worker's compensation, weather, animal mortality, cast/models, and umbrella liability.

Fees: $275 annual general membership.

Info by Art Form – Photography

pARTS Photographic Arts

711 Lake St. W, Minneapolis, MN 55408
Phone: 612-824-5500 Email: parts@bitstream.net
Fax: 612-824-5511 Website: www.partsphoto.org

Services: pARTs Photographic Arts is a nonprofit photography gallery and resource center in Minneapolis. pARTs mission is to build a community that supports excellence in photography and to engage and nurture a broad audience for photography through a program of exhibitions, dialogues, publications, and outreach.

Education: pARTs provides classes for elementary students in South Minneapolis through their Youth Arts Experience program and one-on-one mentoring with area high school students. Adult classes on various topics are also offered.

Fees: Exhibitions and openings are free. Fees vary for other events with discounts for members.

Professional Photographers of America

Phone: 404-522-8600 Email: csc@ppa.com
Toll-Free: 800-786-6277 Website: www.ppa.com

Services: PPA is the world's leading certifying agency for imaging professionals and the world's largest nonprofit association for professional photographers. PPA offers consumers free referrals to photographic professionals, as well as acting as a locator service for finding the owners of images. PPA members can receive equipment and health insurance.

Vision Quest Photographic Arts Center

2370 Hendon Ave., St. Paul, MN 55108-1453
Phone: 651-644-1400 Email: beasley@bitstream.net
Fax: 651-644-8777 Website: www.VQphoto.com

Services: The Center offers photography workshops that emphasize content and creativity over the mechanics of camera use. The organization is committed to being a nonprofit, affordable arts education center for photographers, artists, teachers, and students in an equal opportunity atmosphere.

Info by Art Form – Photography/Website Construction

Vision Quest, cont.

Education: Vision Quest provides workshops, retreats, and international study trips.

Fees: $295 including food and lodging for a 3-day weekend workshop, more for longer workshops.

Women in Photography and Visual Arts
See page 35

Women Photographers and Visual Artists (WPVA)
8965 80th St. S, Cottage Grove, MN 55016
Phone: 651-459-2725   Email: cjbracci@tcinternet.net
Fax: 612-729-0460

Services: WPVA provides members with networking, exhibition opportunities, and monthly meetings. Presents frequent subject or interest programs at monthly meetings.

Fees: $30/individual, $15/full-time student annual membership.

Website Construction

Migizi – National Native Information Center
3123 Lake St. E, Minneapolis, MN 55406-2028
Phone: 612-721-6631, ext. 200   Email: postmaster@nnic.com
Fax: (612) 721-3936   Website: www.nnic.com
                                  or: www.migizi.org

Services: MIGIZI Communications is a nonprofit organization providing services to the American Indian community. Its National Native Information Center provides custom web development for nonprofits and small businesses, network and web development training, general computer training, and technology consulting.

Info by Art Form – Website Construction/Crafts

TwinCitiesArtists.com
1919 Seventh St. S, Minneapolis, MN 55454
Phone: 612-339-5027   Email: info@TwinCitiesArtists.com
                          Website: TwinCitiesArtists.com

Services: TwinCitiesArtists.com is a group of Internet-friendly Twin Cities artists who want to promote art in the Twin Cities area by building professional websites for artists, galleries, art organizations, music venues, and art shops at prices they can afford.

Crafts

American Craft Council
72 Spring St., Sixth Fl., New York, NY 10012-4019
Phone: 212-274-0630   Email: council@craftcouncil.org
Fax: 212-274-0650   Website: www.craftcouncil.org
Toll-Free: 800-724-0859

Services: The American Craft Council is a national, nonprofit educational organization with a mission to foster an environment in which craft is understood and valued. The Council's programs include the bimonthly magazine *American Craft*, eleven annual craft shows and markets, a special library on contemporary crafts, education, grants, workshops, and seminars, as well as services to professional craftspeople and retailers. Membership in the Council is open to all.

Fees: $40 annual membership.

Midwest Art Fairs Directory
See page 5.

Info by Art Form — Crafts /Ceramics

Minnesota Crafts Council

528 Hennepin Ave. S, Suite 216, Minneapolis, MN 55403

Phone: 612-333-7789　　　　Email: mncraft@mtn.org

Fax: 612-332-8131　　　　　Website: www.mncraft.org

Toll-Free: 888-805-1068

Services: MCC is a regional arts organization promoting excellence in craft media and appreciation of the handmade object. The council provides a communications network for craft artists and sponsors the Minnesota Crafts Festival (at the College of St. Catherine) and the Fiber/Metal Arts Show annually. They hold an annual members' exhibit and provide other retail venues for member artists as they come available.

Education: An annual conference each January, co-sponsored artist and business development workshops throughout the year.

Fees: Vary by level of membership.

Ceramics

Northern Clay Center

2424 Franklin Ave. E, Minneapolis, MN 55406

Phone: 612-339-8007　　　　Website: www.northernclaycenter.org

Fax: 612-339-0592

Services: The goals of the Center are to promote excellence in the work of clay artists, to provide educational opportunities for artists and the community, and to encourage and expand the public's appreciation and understanding of all forms of the ceramic arts. The Center offers classes, a variety of exhibitions throughout the year, and retail services.

Education: Classes are offered year-round, from beginning to advanced levels, on a quarterly basis. Summer day clay camps are offered for children, and special workshops are held for adults, children, and families.

Fees: Vary by class.

Info by Art Form – Fiber Arts & Textiles

Fiber Arts & Textiles

American Sewing Guild, Minnesota Chapter

LaVerne Bell, PO Box 21214, Minneapolis, MN 55421-0421

Phone: 612-339-5568 (Twin Cities) Email: lucasruth@yahoo.com

218-628-2952 (Duluth)   Website: www.asg.org

816-444-3500 (National)

Services: American Sewing Guild is a group of home sewers providing information, education, retreats, and programs in the spirit of sewing.

Associated Sewing

690 Snelling Ave. N, St. Paul, MN 55104

Phone: 651-645-9449   Email: AssocSew@aol.com

Fax: 651-641-0391   Website: www.associatedsewing.com

Services: Associated Sewing has five local stores, offers sewing/embroidery/computer design classes, seminars and retreats, publishes a newsletter four times per year, and hosts a variety of sewing clubs.

Costume Guild of Minnesota

Concordia University, 275 Syndicate N, St. Paul, MN 55104

Phone: 651-641-8891

Services: The Costume Guild of Minnesota is dedicated to building a group network that provides resources, knowledge, and support for its members. Meetings are once a month.

Fees: $50/family or corporate, $30/individual, $20/student, $5/newsletter only annual membership. Non-members pay a $3 fee to attend programs.

Handweavers Guild of America

Two Executive Concourse, Suite 201, 3327 Duluth Hwy, Duluth, GA 30096-3301

Phone: 770-495-7702   Email: weavespindye@compuserve.com

Fax: 770-495-7703   Website: www.weavespindye.org

Services: The Handweavers Guild of America, Inc., is dedicated to inspiring creativity and preserving fiber traditions through education. It

Handweavers' Guild of America, cont.

accomplishes this by providing forums for the education of handweavers, handspinners, basketmakers, and fiber artists in related disciplines.

Fees: $45 annual membership.

Minnesota Basket Weavers Guild

Phone: 651-484-7409   Email: lkallevig@isd.net

Services: Guest teachers instruct on the last Saturday of each month for all levels of basket making. Weekend workshops are also held regularly.

Education: Certain Guild members are available for teaching the art of basket making in the schools.

Fees: $20 annual membership.

Minnesota Contemporary Quilters

5044 Fremont Ave. S, Minneapolis, MN 55419

Phone: 612-827-3415   Email: PORCURTIS@aol.com

Services: Education, exploration, and support in the art of quilting. Meeting are held every other month.

Fees: $15 annual membership.

Minnesota Knitters' Guild

PO Box 75184, St. Paul, MN 55175

Phone: 651-298-9072

Services: The Minnesota Knitters' Guild holds meetings on the third Tuesday of each month (7:00-9:00 p.m.) at the College of St. Catherine's Mendel Hall. The Guild also has a library, quarterly newsletter, and knitting contests.

Fees: $18 annual membership includes credit toward the annual Yarn-over.

Info by Art Form – Fiber Arts & Textiles

Minnesota Lace Society

PO Box 2671, St. Paul, MN 55102

Phone: 651-257-1388

Services: The Society conducts meetings, publishes a monthly newsletter, has a resource library, and access to supplies and equipment. They offer a statewide network of artists, designers, and collectives, in addition to coordinating national and international networks for their members.

Education: Workshops, demonstrations, and conferences.

Minnesota Quilters, Inc.

1399 Eustis St., St. Paul, MN 55108

Phone: 651-642-9538   Email: quilter@mnquilt.org

Fax: 419-821-3988   Website: www.mnquilt.org

Services: Minnesota Quilters, Inc. is a nonprofit organization dedicated to advancing the love and lore of quilting in the state of Minnesota. Minnesota Quilters' mission is to further the preservation of quilting, to educate, and document the art and craft of quilting in Minnesota. The Quilters have meetings, quilt shows, a resource library, workshops, an annual exhibition and conference.

Education: Workshops throughout the year and at the annual conference.

Fees: $20 annual membership.

Minnesota Valley Fiber Arts Guild

c/o Cindy Graff, 2836 Webster Ave. S, St. Louis Park, MN 55416

Phone: 952-929-6811

Services: The Guild works to promote the understanding and enjoyment of fiber-related areas.

Fees: $20 annual membership.

Needlework Guild of Minnesota

PO Box 16506, St. Louis Park, MN 55416

Phone: 651-437-469   Email: webmistress@needleworkguildmn.org

(Mary Kay Gergen, President)   Website: www.needleworkguildmn.org

Info by Art Form – Fiber Arts & Textiles

Needlework Guild of Minnesota, cont.

Services: The Needlework Guild offers monthly programs of education and study in the practice of various needlework techniques. They also have a circulating library on a variety of sewing topics, and publish six newsletters each year.

Education: The Guild contracts with a variety of national and local teachers each year to give lectures, seminars, and one to four day workshops on a variety of needlework interests. They also have an annual retreat, with the option of independent study.

Fees: $25 annual membership.

St. Paul Needleworkers Guild

6037 Woodale Ave. S, Edina, MN 55424

Phone: 651-644-3606   Email: webmistress@stpaulneedleworkers.org
Website: www.stpaulneedleworkers.org

Services: St. Paul Needleworkers Guild is the local branch of the Embroiderers' Guild of America.

Fees: $32 annual membership.

Textile Center of Minnesota

2324 University Ave. W, Suite 106, St. Paul, MN 55114

Phone: 651-917-7270   Email: mmiller@mtn.org

Fax: 651-917-7271   Website: www.mtn.org/textilecenter/

Services: The Textile Center of Minnesota is a nonprofit organization for shared information, education, and economic opportunities for fiber artists in the Upper Midwest. TCM produces an annual Artwear runway show, members' exhibition, and national juried exhibitions for fiber artists. The Center publishes a quarterly newsletter and a calendar of events which includes textile happenings throughout the state.

Education: Local and nationally reknowned fiber artists are brought in to lecture and give workshops.

Fees: Vary by level of membership.

Info by Art Form – Fiber Arts & Textiles

Textile Council of the Minneapolis Institute of Arts

2400 Third Ave. S, Minneapolis, MN 55404

Phone: 612-870-3047 Website: www.artsMIA.org

Services: The Textile Council promotes individual and community-wide appreciation of the textile arts and also raises funds to purchase textiles for the museum's collection.

Education: The council has sponsors lectures and seminars.

Fees: Vary by level of membership.

Upper Midwest Bead Society

PO Box 4081, St. Paul, MN 55104

Phone: 651-777-5913 Email: beadenvy@prodigy.net

Fax: 651-633-2107 Website: http://members.tripod.com/umbs/

Services: The Bead Society holds monthly meetings which include slide presentations, demonstrations on the various techniques of beading, a "show-and-tell" segment, bead history, and more. Their newsletter contains opportunities, exhibit entries, a review of relevant bead products, updates on new books about beadwork, and general beading information.

Education: Bead camp/retreat.

Weavers' Guild and School of Minnesota

2402 University Ave. W, St. Paul, MN 55114

Phone: 651-644-3594 Email: weaversguild@juno.com

Fax: 651-644-3594

Services: The Guild has an extensive library, a dye studio, and more than 30 floor looms. They offer weaving materials at greatly reduced prices and have a bulletin board where equipment and supplies are listed for sale. The Guild meets monthly from September through May, several study groups provide support and educational opportunities for interested members, and a monthly newsletter is published. A gallery in which members display and sell items has recently been opened and is accessible to the public.

Education: The Guild offers more than 90 classes annually in weaving, spinning, dying, and other fiber crafts, including classes for children.

Fees: $40 annual membership. Membership year is September 1 through August 31 and dues are not prorated.

Music

American Composers Forum
332 Minnesota St., Suite E145, St. Paul, MN 55101-1300
Phone: 651-228-1407   Email: aaa@artswire.org
Fax: 651-291-7978   Website: www.composersforum.org
Services: American Composers Forum seeks to link communities with composers and performers. The Forum develops programs that educate today's and tomorrow's audiences, stimulate entrepreneurship and collaboration, and serve as models of support for the arts.
Fees: Vary by level of membership.

American Music Center
30 26th St. W, Suite 1001, New York, NY 10010-2011
Phone: 212-366-5260 ext. 11   Email: info@amc.net
Fax: 212-366-5265   Website: www.amc.net
On-line magazine: www.NewMusicBox.org
Services: The American Music Center is an information and resource center for contemporary music and jazz.
Education: Professional-development workshops are offered for composers. *New American Music for Young Audiences* is available to Education Directors in catalog form and on web site.
Fees: $55 annual membership.

American Music Therapy Association, Inc. (AMTA)
8455 Colesville Rd., Suite 1000, Silver Spring, MD 20910
Phone: 301-589-3300   Email: info@musictherapy.org
Fax: 301-589-5175   Website: www.musictherapy.org
Services: The purpose of AMTA is to develop the therapeutic use of music in rehabilitation, special education, and community settings. AMTA is committed to the advancement of education, training, professional standards, credentials, and research supporting the music therapy profession.
Fees: $170 annual membership.

Info by Art Form – Music

Chamber Music America

305 Seventh Ave., New York, NY 10001-6008
Phone: 212-242-2022　　　　Email: info@chamber-music.org
Fax: 212-242-7955　　　　　Website: www.chamber-music.org

Services: The mission of Chamber Music America is to develop resources that nurture and support artistic excellence and promote the economic stability of professional chamber music. Their services include six grant programs, technical assistance from CMA program staff, professional development through conferences, workshops, a wide range of publications, advocacy on the national and local level, health and instrument insurance, and long-distance telephone service.

Early Music America

11421 1/2 Bellflower Rd., Cleveland, OH 44106
Phone: 216-229-1685　　　　Email: office@earlymusic.org
Fax: 216-229-1688　　　　　Website: www.earlymusic.org
Toll-Free: 888-722-5288

Services: Early Music America serves and strengthens North America's early music community – including professionals, amateurs, and enthusiasts – and raises public awareness of early music. They provide a quarterly magazine, other publications, insurance programs, and workshops.
Education: Workshops and conferences.
Fees: $45 annual membership.

MacPhail Center for the Arts

1128 LaSalle Ave., Minneapolis, MN 55403
Phone: 612-321-0100　　　　Email: mac@gold.tc.umn.edu
Fax: 612-321-9740　　　　　Website: www.macphail.org

Services: The MacPhail Center is a community resource for education and performance experiences in musical arts for people of all ages, abilities, and economic circumstances.
Education: Music lessons, performance, and master classes.
Fees: Classes and instruction are offered on a sliding fee scale for lower-income persons.

Minneapolis Drum and Dance Center

Cultural Center of Minnesota, 3013 Lyndale Ave. S, Minneapolis, MN 55408

Phone: 612-827-0771

Services: The Center offers classes, workshops, and ensemble groups for percussionists and dancers.

Fees: Class fees vary.

Minnesota Association for Music Therapy

1313 Boyce St., Hopkins, MN 55343

Phone: 952-475-2118

Services: The Minnesota Association for Music Therapy publishes a newsletter twice a year which includes a notification of upcoming workshops. Employment opportunities for therapists are made available through a job hotline.

Fees: $7/student, $15/professional annual membership.

Minnesota Association of Songwriters

PO Box 581816, Minneapolis, MN 55458-1816

Phone: 651-649-4636   Email: mas@mndir.com

Website: www.isc.net/mas/

Services: The MAS is a nonprofit community of songwriters from the Midwest. It's mission is to inspire, educate, and promote the art and craft of songwriting. As a resource, the MAS is a connection between writers, other music-oriented organizations, and the music industry. Meetings are held twice monthly.

Education: Critique nights and craft workshops.

Fees: General membership is free.

Info by Art Form — Music

Minnesota Bluegrass and Old-time Music Association
PO Box 11419, St. Paul, MN 55111-0419
Phone: 612-688-7757   Email: mbotmamail@aol.com
Websites: www.minnesotabluegrass.org or www.minnesotaoldtime.org
Festival line: 800-635-3037

Services: The Minnesota Bluegrass & Old-Time Music Association holds jam sessions, concert events, and three annual bluegrass & old-time music festivals. It publishes a monthly newsletter, *Inside Bluegrass*.

Fees: $20/individual, $25/family, $40/band, $60/sustaining, $120/patron annual membership.

Minnesota Chapter of the Gospel Music Workshop
396 Lexington Pkwy. N, St. Paul, MN 55104
Phone: 651-659-0021

Services: The Workshop holds choral meetings approximately four times per month, and sponsors workshops on technique and musical development. They also publish a bimonthly newsletter.

Fees: $25-$50 annual membership.

Minnesota Guitar Society
PO Box 14986, Minneapolis, MN 55414
Phone: 612-374-4681

Services: The Guitar Society offers monthly forums and a bimonthly newsletter. They also plan concerts and have a sheet music library.
Education: Workshops and lectures.

Minnesota Music Academy
PO Box 2823, Loop Station, Minneapolis, MN 55402
Phone: 612-229-3121   Email: help@minnesotamusicacademy.com
                                   Website: www.bitstream.net/mma

Services: The Minnesota Music Academy (MMA) is a nonprofit corporation committed to assisting Minnesota musicians with their artistic and professional development through programs of education and recognition.

Minnesota Music Academy, cont.

Education: Educational seminars for the Minnesota music community are held approximately every two months. Seminars presented by other local associations are also listed at MMA.

Fees: $15/individual, $100/patron annual membership.

Minnesota Music Directory

City Pages, 401 Third St. N, #550, Minneapolis, MN 55401
Phone: 612-375-1015   Website: www.citypages.com/mmd/
Fax: 612-372-3737

Services: The Directory includes listings of agents and management, artists, equipment sales and service, performance venues, instruction, radio stations, record producers, studios, record companies, video production companies, rehearsal spaces, and more.

Musician's Assistance Program

PO Box 272, Excelsior, MN 55331
Phone: 952-401-8842
Toll-Free: 888-627-6271

Services: The Program helps individuals within the music community recover from drug and alcohol abuse.

Percussive Arts Society, Minnesota Chapter

c/o Peter O'Gorman, 2224 Third St., White Bear Lake, MN 55110
Phone: 651-429-4763   Email: percarts@pas.org
                              Website: www.pas.org/Chapters/Minnesota/

Services: The Percussive Arts Society (PAS®) is a nonprofit service organization. Its purpose is educational, promoting drums and percussion through a viable network of performers, teachers, students, enthusiasts, and sustaining members. Health insurance benefits included in membership.

Education: Annual Percussive Arts Society International Convention (PASIC®); four days of clinics, master classes, concerts, workshops, Marching Percussion Festival, and exhibit hall.

Fees: $35/student, $55/professional annual membership.

Info by Art Form – Music

Twin Cities Jazz Society

PO Box 4487, St. Paul, MN 55104
Phone: 651-633-0329   Email: tcjs@mtn.org
Fax: 612-663-3134   Website: mtn.org/TCJS/main.html

Services: The Twin Cities Jazz Society (TCJS) is a nonprofit, all volunteer organization dedicated to promoting jazz music in all of its forms. TCJS sponsors concerts, workshops, and education programs in area schools and we have just begun a new scholarship program to help rising young local talent. Much effort of the Society is put into their newsletter *JazzNotes*.

Fees: $15/student, $35/family, $25/individual annual membership.

Twin Cities Musicians Union

Local 30-73 AFM Machinist's Labor Temple
1399 Eustis St., Suite 202, St. Paul, MN 55108-1546
Phone: 651-646-7829   Email: tcmu@isd.net
Fax: 651-646-2088   Website: www.tcmu.com

Services: There are 2000 members in the Twin Cities Musicians Union, a chapter of the American Federation of Musicians. Health insurance is offered through the Union.

Fees: Annual membership.

Upper Mississippi Blues Society

9800 Redwood St. NW, #204, Coon Rapids, MN 55433
Phone: 763-755-2617

Services: The Blues Society holds an annual blues festival, has workshops throughout the year, and publishes a newsletter containing news, events, and networking/contact information.

West Bank School of Music

See page 29

Theater & Performance

Actors' Equity Association Hotline

4408 Washburn Ave. S, Minneapolis, MN 55410

Phone: 612-924-4044 Website: www.actorsequity.org

Services: This information line has regional audition information and other information for actors and equity members.

The Dramatists Guild of America

1501 Broadway, Suite 701, New York, NY 10036

Phone: 212-398-9366 Email: Igor@Dramaguild.com

Fax: 212-944-0420 Website: www.dramaguild.com

Services: The Dramatists Guild of America is the only professional association for playwrights, composers, and lyricists. Members of the Dramatists Guild have access to two health and dental insurance programs and a group term life insurance plan.

Fees: $35/student, $75/associate, $125/active annual membership.

Minnesota Association of Community Theatres

245 Cedar Ave., Minneapolis, MN 55454

Phone: 651-644-1187(general) Email: mactfacts@aol.com
       612-521-5692(hotline) Website: www.mact.net

Fax: 651-644-2679

Toll-Free: 800-290-2428

Services: The Minnesota Association of Community Theatres (MACT) is a service organization presenting play festivals, conferences, workshops, meetings, newsletters, a theater hotline, and other resources.

Education: Occasional theater-related workshops and conferences.

Info by Art Form – Theater & Performance

The Playwrights' Center

2301 Franklin Ave. E, Minneapolis, MN 55406-1099
Phone: 612-332-7481   Email: pwcenter@mtn.org
Fax: 612-332-6037   Website: www.pwcenter.org

Services: The Playwrights' Center is a regional and national resource for script development which caters to writers at all stages of their careers and provides a range of services including: public readings, private workshops, classes, conferences, roundtables, residencies, and fellowships.

Education: Lectures, seminars, discussions, classes, and workshops.

Fees: $20/student, $40/individual annual membership.

Screen Actors Guild (SAG)

American Federation of Television and Radio Artists
798 First St. N, Suite 333, Minneapolis, MN 55401
Phone: 612-371-9120   Email: saginfo@sag.org
Fax: 612-371-9119   Website: www.sag.org

Services: SAG is a performers' union, representing actors, voice-over artists, dancers, and singers. Job opportunities are posted online.

Theater Communications Group

355 Lexington Ave., New York, NY 10017-0217
Phone: 212-697-5230   Email: tcg@tcg.org
Fax: 212-983-4847   Website: www.tcg.org

Services: Theatre Communications Group (TCG), the national organization for the American theater, offers a wide array of services in line with their mission to promote the nonprofit American theater.

Fees: $30/individual annual membership.

Dance

American Dance Therapy Association, MN Chapter
4350 Reiland Ln., Shoreview, MN 55126
Phone: 651-721-6642   Email: info@adta.org
Fax: 651-721-6642   Website: www.adta.org

Services: American Dance Therapy Association works to establish and maintain high standards of professional education and competence in the field of dance/movement therapy. Their publications include the *ADTA Newsletter*, the *American Journal of Dance Therapy*, monographs, and conference proceedings.

Education: ADTA holds an annual conference and supports formation of regional groups, conferences, seminars, workshops, and meetings.

Ballet Arts Minnesota
528 Hennepin Ave. S, Suite 201, Minneapolis, MN 55403
Phone: 612-340-1071   Email: dancebam@mtn.org
Fax: 612-332-8131   Website: www.balletartsminnesota.org

Services: Ballet Arts Minnesota cultivates and advances ballet in the region through education and performance in traditional and contemporary forms, and is the home of the City Children's Nutcracker.

Education: Training and performance experience for children ages 4-8, youth ages 8-18, and adults.

Fees: Discounts to seniors, students, and MN Dance Alliance members. Limited partial scholarships are available.

Minnesota Ballet
301 First St. W, Suite 800, Duluth, MN 55802
Phone: 218-529-3742   Email: info@minnesotaballet.org
Fax: 218-529-3744   Website: www.minnesotaballet.org/school/

Services: Classes are offered for all ages, 3 to adult in creative movement, ballet, young men's, modern, jazz, ballroom, and creative dance for the physically challenged.

Fees: Call for schedule and fees.

Info by Art Form — Dance

Minnesota Dance Alliance

528 Hennepin Ave. S, Suite 600, Minneapolis, MN 55403-1804

Phone: 612-340-1900

Fax: 612-340-9919

Services: The Minnesota Dance Alliance, located in the Hennepin Center for the Arts Building, is a service organization that aims to transform the environment for dance. From its start, the organization has championed local dance artists by presenting their work.

Fees: $20 newsletter subscription, $25 discount card.

Minnesota Dance Theatre & School

528 Hennepin Ave. S, Fifth Fl., Minneapolis, MN 55403

Phone: 612-338-0627   Website: www.mndance.org

Fax: 612-338-5160

Services: This ballet school teaches students, ages three to adult, and presents lecture-demonstrations and three dance concerts per year.

The Watson/Ragmala Dance Center

711 Lake St. W, Suite 308, Minneapolis, MN 55408

Phone: 612-825-6624

Services: The Watson/Ragmala Dance Center offers classes in modern, ballet, and Alexander technique. Studio space is available for rental.

Fees: Vary depending on class.

Zenon Dance Company and School

528 Hennepin Ave. S, Suite 400, Minneapolis, MN 55403

Phone: 612-338-1101

Fax: 612-338-2479

Services: Zenon Dance School offers classes in modern, jazz, ballet, hip-hop, African, yoga, and pilates to students of all ages, including a multicultural dance program for lower-income children. The Company performs locally, nationally, and internationally.

Storytelling

Black Storytellers Alliance
1112 Newton Ave. N, Minneapolis, MN 55411
Phone: 612-529-5864   Email: nzulu@blackstorytellers.com
Fax: 612-529-5864   Website: www.blackstorytellers.com

Services: The main goal of Black Storytellers Alliance is to promote and preserve the art of storytelling. The group specializes in storytelling performances for schools, libraries, community centers, and corporations. Members of BSA do school residencies and provide instructional workshops for teachers, librarians, parents, and volunteers. BSA also provides limited internships.

Education: BSA provides workshops and also produces the annual "Signifyin' & Testifyin'" storytelling festival.

Fees: $15/general, $30/practitioner annual membership.

Northlands Storytelling Network
PO Box 1437, Minnetonka, MN 55345
Phone: 952-934-4194   Email: northlands@aol.com
Fax: 952-937-9643

Services: The Network is an advocacy group which publishes a newsletter, holds an annual conference, and is a resource for all other storytelling groups and events in town.

Fees: $20 annual membership.

Storyfront
Bethany Lutheran Church, 2511 Franklin Ave. E, Minneapolis, MN 55406

Services: Storyfront holds meetings with a speaker and test-storytelling sessions (with feedback) monthly. They also sponsor weekly storytelling sessions on Fridays.

Writing & Literature

The Authors Guild
330 W 42nd St. 29th Fl., New York, NY 10036
Phone: 212-563-5904   Email: staff@authorsguild.org
Fax: 212-564-5363   Website: www.authorsguild.org
Services: The Authors Guild is the nation's largest society of published authors, and is an advocate for free speech, fair compensation, and copyright protection. The Authors League Fund offers interest-free loans to professional, published writers and playwrights.

Children's Book Illustrators Guild
See page 41.

The Loft Literary Center
Open Book, 1011 Washington Ave. S, Suite 200, Minneapolis, MN 55415
Phone: 612-215-2575   Email: loft@loft.org
Fax: 612-215-2576   Website: www.loft.org
Services: The Loft is the nation's largest, most comprehensive literary center. The mission of the Loft is to foster a writing community, the artistic development of individual writers, and an audience for literature. The Loft offers creative writing courses, grants, mentorship programs, and public events.
Education: Classes and workshops feature writers of local, national, and international stature.
Fees: $40/individual, $50/household annual membership. For creative writing courses, a sliding fee scale dependent upon household income and membership status.

Minneapolis Writers' Workshop
PO Box 24356, Minneapolis, MN 55424
Services: The Workshop holds weekly meetings which include readings and critiques. They also host an annual writers' conference.
Fees: $20 annual membership.

Info by Art Form – Writing & Literature

Minnesota Literature

1 Nord Cir., St. Paul, MN 55127
Phone: 651-483-3904   Email: Mnlit@aol.com
Fax: 651-766-0144

Services: This monthly newsletter for writers provides a calendar of events, news on the writing market, and opportunities for writers (including publication contacts, workshops, contests, grants, classes, and awards). They also publish a biennial bibliography of Minnesota publishers and publications of literature.

Minnesota Society of Children's Book Writers and Illustrators

See page 42.

National Association for Poetry Therapy (NAPT)

5505 Connecticut Ave. NW, #280, Washington, DC 20015
Phone: 202-966-2536   Email: rdaniel@his.com
                           Website: www.poetrytherapy.org

Services: The NAPT is a community of people who share a love for the use of language arts in growth and healing. Members represent a wide range of professional experience, schools of therapy, educational affiliations, artistic disciplines, and other fields of training in both mental and physical health. Members receive a newsletter, *The Museletter*, published by NAPT, and the quarterly *Journal of Poetry Therapy*, published by Plenum Press.

Fees: $65/student, $100/professional annual membership.

National Writers Union

PO Box 50507, Minneapolis, MN 55403
Phone: 612-879-5572 (local chapter)
Phone: 212-254-0279 (National)   Email: nwu@nwu.org
Fax: 212-254-0673   Website: www.nwu.org

Services: The National Writers Union (NWU) is the trade union for freelance writers of all genres who work for American publishers or employers. The Union offers grievance resolution, industry campaigns,

Info by Art Form – Writing & Literature

National Writers Union, cont.

contract advice, health & dental plans, member education, job banks, networking, social events, and much more.

Education: Panel discussions and forums.

Fees: Membership fees depend on writing income.

P.E.N. Writers Fund

P.E.N. American Center, 568 Broadway, New York, NY 10012
Phone: 212-334-1660   Email: pen@pen.org
Fax: 212-334-2181   Website: www.pen.org

Services: The PEN Writers Fund is an emergency fund for professional (published or produced) writers with serious financial difficulties. Depending on the situation, the fund gives grants or loans up to $1000.

The Playwrights' Center

See page 62.

SASE: The Write Place

711 Lake St. W, Suite 211, Minneapolis, MN 55408
Phone: 612-822-2500   Email: sase@mtn.org
Fax: 612-822-0095   Website: www.mtn.org/sase
TTY: 612-822-2500

Services: SASE provides affordable programming, administered by a diverse group of people, for writers of all backgrounds to develop their craft and present or publish their works.

Education: SASE offers workshops and mentorships. Please check the website or contact SASE for more information.

Screenwriters Workshop

868 19th Ave. SE, Minneapolis, MN 55458-0800

Phone: 612-331-3880

Services: The Workshop publishes *Screenline*, a quarterly newsletter with articles and opportunities. It also provides script consulting, reading and writing groups, and a public reading series.

Education: Workshops and screen labs.

Book & Paper Arts

Colleagues of Calligraphy

PO Box 4024, St. Paul, MN 55104

Phone: 612-722-1429   Email: beerykat@uswest.net

Services: Meets eight times per year and holds demonstrations, lectures, exhibits, workshops, and conferences. An International Conference of Lettering Artists will be hosted by the Colleagues of Calligraphy in Summer of 2002 at St. John's University.

Fees: $25 annual membership.

Hand Papermaking, Inc.

PO Box 77027, Washington, DC 20013-7027

Phone: 301-220-2393   Email: handpapermaking@bookarts.com

Fax: 301-220-2394

Toll-Free: 800-821-6604

Website: www.bookarts.com/handpapermaking

Services: Hand Papermaking, Inc. is a nonprofit organization dedicated to advancing traditional and contemporary ideas in the art of hand papermaking through publications and other means.

Minnesota Center for Book Arts (MCBA)

Open Book, 1011 Washington Ave. S, Suite 100, Minneapolis, MN 55415
Phone: 612-338-3634   Email: mcba@mnbookarts.org
Fax: 612-338-1562   Website: www.mnbookarts.org

Services: The Minnesota Center for Book Arts' mission is to advance the book as a vital contemporary art form, preserving the traditional crafts of bookmaking and engaging people in learning, production, interpretive, and collaborative experiences. Offers artist residencies.

Education: Lectures and classes.

Grants, Funds and Employment

Artist Grants & Fellowships	72
Artist Residencies	77
Artist Loans	79
Small Business Loans	79
Housing Loans	80
Emergency Funds	83
Employment	86

Artist Grants & Fellowships

American Composers Forum
See page 55.

Art Matters
PO Box 1815, New York, NY 10113-1815

Services: Art Matters provides critical needs funding and fellowships for photographers living with HIV/AIDS. Process time for applications is up to one month.

Blacklock Nature Sanctuary Artist Fellowship Program
PO Box 426, Moose Lake, MN 55767-0426

Phone: 612-823-6257   Email: jorda021@tc.umn.edu
Fax: 612-823-2637   Website: www.blacklock.org

Services: Blacklock Nature Sanctuary, located near Moose Lake, Minnesota, offers two studios and 400 acres of woodlands and lakeshore to artists and naturalists in residence. The Artist Fellowship Program funded by the Jerome Foundation supports emerging artists with a stipend and uninterrupted time in a quiet, natural setting to initiate or develop an artistic project. The Nadine Blacklock Nature Photography Fellowship supports one woman nature photographer from anywhere and at any career level for a one month residency with stipend.

Fees: There is no fee to apply for the fellowships. The Blacklock Nature Sanctuary is also available to rent by the weekend, week, or month when not being used by selected artists. Check the website for fees.

Bush Artist Fellows Program
E-900 First National Bank Building, 332 Minnesota St., St. Paul, MN 55101

Phone: 651-227-5222   Fax: 651-292-4315

Services: The Bush Artist Fellowships provide artists with significant financial support that enables them to further their work and their contribution to their communities.

Foundation Center

79 Fifth Ave., New York, NY 10003
Phone: 212-620-4230   Email: feedback@fdncenter.org
Fax: 212-691-1828   Website: www.fdncenter.org
Services: The Foundation Center helps connect grant seekers and grantmakers.

The Foundation Center Cooperating Collection

Minneapolis Public Library, 300 Nicollet Mall, Minneapolis, MN 55401
Phone: 612-372-6555
Fax: 612-372-6546
Services: The Collection has national directories and information on grants to individual artists, foundations, and corporate giving programs, as well as Minnesota fundraising information, computer searches of grants and foundations, free orientation sessions, and telephone reference assistance.
Fees: All services are free.

Grants: A Basic Guide to Grants for Minnesota Artists

RCA, 308 Prince St., Suite 270, St. Paul, MN 55101
Phone: 651-292-4381   Email: info@rc4arts.org
Fax: 651-292-4315   Website: www.rc4arts.org
TTY: 651-292-3218
Services: *Grants* provides a listing of fellowship and project assistance grants, contact information, and general descriptions of grantmaking organizations.
Fees: Copies free at RCA or Minnesota State Arts Board. Downloadable version available at MSAB website (www.arts.state.mn.us).

Intermedia Arts

See page 4.

Grants, Funds & Employment – Artist Grants & Fellowships

Jerome Foundation

125 Park Square Court, 400 Sibley St., St. Paul, MN 55101-1928
Phone: 651-224-9431 Email: info@jeromefdn.org
Fax: 651-224-3439 Website: www.jeromefdn.org
Toll-Free: 800-995-3766

Services: The Jerome Foundation supports programs in dance, literature, media arts, music, theater, performance art, visual arts, multidisciplinary work, and arts criticism. The Foundation is concerned with providing financial assistance to emerging creative artists of promise, most often assisted through programs operated by nonprofit, tax-exempt organizations. Within each arts discipline, the Foundation focuses on artists who are living and working in Minnesota or New York City.

The Loft Literary Center

See page 66.

The McKnight Foundation

121 Eighth St. S, Suite 600, Minneapolis, MN 55402
Phone: 612-333-4220 Email: ncuthbert@mcknight.org
Fax: 612-317-0766 Website: www.mcknight.org

Services: The arts program seeks to improve the quality of the arts in Minnesota and to improve access to the arts for all citizens of the state. The Foundation commits an average of $8 to $10 million a year to artists, arts organizations, and its fellowship programs. For individual artists, the Foundation's fellowship programs are administered by a variety of artist service organizations and several of the regional arts councils. The Foundation directly administers an annual Distinguished Artist Award.

Grants, Funds & Employment – Artist Grants & Fellowships

Minnesota Council on Foundations
15 Fifth St., Suite 600, Minneapolis, MN 55402-1570
Phone: 612-338-1989   Email: info@mcf.org
Fax: 612-337-5089   Website: www.mcf.org
Services: This association of foundations and corporate grantmakers offers workshops, publishes information on Minnesota grantmaking, and researches Minnesota grantmaking trends and patterns.
Education: Conduct quarterly "Grantsmanship for Beginners" workshops on the basics of grantseeking.

Minnesota Literature
See page 67.

Minnesota State Arts Board
See page 11.

National Endowment for the Arts
110 Pennsylvania Ave. NW, Washington, DC 20506
Phone: 202-682-5786   Email: webmgr@arts.endow.gov
Fax: 202-682-5002   Website: www.endow.gov
Services: The National Endowment for the Arts provides organizational grants as well as grants for individual writers and jazz musicians. They also offer Arts Administration internships.

National Foundation for Advancement of the Arts
800 Brickell Ave., Suite 500, Miami, FL 33131
Phone: 305-377-1140   Email: nfaa@nfaa.org
Fax: 305-377-1149   Website: www.nfaa.org
Toll-Free: 800-970-ARTS
Services: The NFAA supports young and emerging artists with career grants, residencies, and scholarships.

Grants, Funds & Employment - Artist Grants & Fellowships

National Sculpture Society
See page 37.

P.E.N. Fund for Writers and Editors with HIV/AIDS
P.E.N. American Center, 568 Broadway, New York, NY 10012
Phone: 212-334-1660   Email: pen@pen.org
Fax: 212-334-2181   Website: www.pen.org

Services: This fund gives grants of up to $1000 to professional writers and editors who face serious financial difficulties because of HIV or AIDS-related illness.

The Playwrights' Center
See page 62.

The Pollock-Krasner Foundation, Inc.
863 Park Ave., New York, NY 10021
Phone: 212-517-5400   Email: grants@pkf.org
Fax: 212-288-2836   Website: www.pkf.org

Services: The Pollock-Krasner Foundation, Inc. was established for the purpose of providing financial assistance to individual visual artists of established ability.

Regional Arts Councils Providing Grants & Fellowships

Arrowhead Regional Arts Council (Region 3)
See page 12.

Lake Region Arts Council (Region 4)
See page 12.

Five Wings Arts Council (Region 5)
See page 13.

East Central Arts Council (Region 7E)
See page 14.

The Central Minnesota Arts Board (Region 7W)
See page 14.

Prairie Lakes Regional Arts Council (Region 9)
See page 14.

Artist Residencies

The Anderson Center at Tower View
PO Box 406, Red Wing, MN 55066
Phone: 651-388-2009   Email: acis@pressenter.com
                             Website: www.pressenter.com/~acis/
Services: The Anderson Center brings in emerging and established artists, scientists, and humanists to their residency program.
Fees: $15 non-refundable application fee.

Ethnic Dance Theater
2337 Central Ave. NE, Minneapolis, MN 55418
Phone: 612-782-3970   Email: edt@tcfreenet.org
Fax: 612-782-3977   Website: tcfreenet.org/org/edt/
Services: The Ethnic Dance Theater is a performing arts ensemble celebrating and preserving the dynamic traditional dance and music of diverse world cultures. The Theater provides residencies throughout the year at area schools.

Grants, Funds & Employment - Artist Grants & Fellowships

Intermedia Arts
See page 4.

John Michael Kohler Arts Center
See page 17.

Minnesota Center for Book Arts
See page 70.

New York Mills Arts Retreat & Regional Cultural Center
24 Main Ave. N, PO Box 246, New York Mills, MN 56567
Phone: 218-385-3339   Email: nymills@uslink.net
Fax: 218-385-3366   Websites: www.think-off.org
Toll-Free: 888-877-1969   and: www.kulcher.org

Services: The New York Mills Arts Retreat is a residency program that provides a taste small town life. It immerses artists in the culture of rural Minnesota, while providing ample time and privacy for concentrated work. Visiting artists are expected to spend a small portion of their residency time working with the community and/or schools. The Cultural Center presents art gallery exhibits, performances, and maintains a Sculpture Park.

Education: Art Education kits available to area schools; school tours of gallery; visiting artist residencies and workshops; annual elementary art show.

The Playwrights' Center
See page 62.

Vision Quest Photographic Arts Center
See page 46.

Artist Loans

Resources and Counseling for the Arts
308 Prince St., Suite 270, St. Paul, MN 55101
Phone: 651-292-4381 Email: info@rc4arts.org
Fax: 651-292-4315 Website: www.rc4arts.org
TTY: 651-292-3218

Services: RCA administers the Dayton Hudson Artist Loan Fund, a community-based revolving loan fund designed to serve the needs of Twin Cities artists, especially those who are having a difficult time securing loans from traditional lending sources. To be eligible, artists must live in the seven-county metro area and demonstrate ongoing commitment to their art work. RCA provides business and management training to recipients.

Saint Paul Planning and Economic Development
1300 City Hall Annex, 25 Fourth St. W, St. Paul, MN 55102
Phone: 651-266-6628 Website: www.stpaul.gov/depts/ped/index.html
Fax: 651-228-3261

Services: The PED offers loan packaging/funding for small businesses that fit the cultural development goals that the PED has for different St. Paul neighborhoods. Their Arts and Economic Development Fund provides small operating grants for small and medium sized arts organizations.

Small Business Loans

Minneapolis Community Development Agency
Crown Roller Mill, 105 Fifth Ave. S, Suite 200, Minneapolis, MN 55401
Phone: 612-673-5018 Email: Dawn.Hagen@mcda.org
Fax: 612-673-5113 Website: www.mcda.org

Services: The MCDA is the housing and economic redevelopment arm of the City of Minneapolis. They provide funding and programs for: affordable housing, business growth to provide jobs to Minneapolis

Grants, Funds & Employment - Small Business Loans/Housing Loans

Minneapolis Community Development Agency., cont.

citizens, and neighborhood stabilization and revitalization. In addition to participating financially in the arts, the MCDA often provides technical assistance to arts organizations and individual artists looking for space, seeking financing and/or fundraising help, or needing assistance with organizational or project development or business expansion.

United States Small Business Administration

Mail Code 0508, 610-C Butler Sq., 100 Sixth St. N, Minneapolis, MN 55403
Phone: 612-370-2337   Website: www.sba.gov

Services: SBA provides loans and venture capital financing to small businesses unable to secure financing through normal lending channels. They also offer counseling, workshops, classes, and special assistance for people interested in starting up their own small business.

Housing Loans

Metropolitan Council

Mears Park Center, 230 Fifth St. E, St. Paul, MN 55101
Phone: 651-602-1000   Email: data.center@metc.state.mn.us
Fax: 651-602-1550   Website: www.metrocouncil.org
TTY: 651-291-0904

Services: Plans for the future of the seven-county metropolitan area. Provides printed information on population, housing, and a consumer's guide. Provides Section 8 rent assistance and housing rehabilitation loans. Publishes *Metro Monitor*.

Minneapolis Community Development Agency
See page 79.

Minnesota Housing Finance Agency
400 Sibley St., Suite 300, St. Paul, MN 55101
Phone: 651-296-7608   Email: mhfa@state.mn.us
Fax: 651-296-8139   Website: www.mhfa.state.mn.us
Toll-Free: 800-657-3769
TTY: 651-297-2361

Services: The MHFA is a resource for 40 different housing assistance programs run through both private lending institutions and neighborhood councils throughout the state for low and moderate income persons. Their services include home improvement and purchase loans below the market rate, rental information, and available grants.

Minnesota Valley Action Council
410 Jackson St., PO Box3327, Mankato, MN 56002-3327
Phone: 507-345-6822   Email: lynn@mvac.mankato.mn.us
Fax: 507-345-2414   Website: www.mnvac.org
Toll-Free: 800-767-7139

Services: MVAC is a private, nonprofit organization that uses federal, state, and local resources to provide assistance wherever needed. Programs include emergency assistance, youth services, family and housing loans, employment searches, and work preparation.

Saint Paul Planning and Economic Development
See page 79.

Grants, Funds & Employment - Housing Loans

United Way First Call for Help – Minneapolis Branch
404 Eighth St. S, Minneapolis, MN 55404-1084
Phone: 651-291-0211 Email: FirstCallNet.Online@uwmsp.org
Fax: 612-340-7675 Website: www.firstcallnet.org

Services: First Call For Help is a comprehensive information and referral service that links people in need with appropriate human service providers. It offers free, confidential information on social service, financial management, health, educational programs, and recreational resources.

United Way First Call for Help – St. Paul Branch
100 Robert St. S, St. Paul, MN 55106
Phone: 651-291-0211 Email: FirstCallNet.Online@uwmsp.org
TTY: 651-291-8430 Website: www.uwmsp.org

Services: First Call For Help is a comprehensive information and referral service that links people in need with appropriate human service providers. It offers free, confidential information on social service, financial management, health, educational programs, and recreational resources.

USDA, Rural Development
375 Jackson St., 410 Farm Credit Building, St. Paul, MN 55101
Phone: 651-602-7800 Email: gary.decramer@mn.USDA.gov
Fax: 651-602-7824

Services: Loans are available to purchase houses, for rental properties, or building renovation in areas of rural Minnesota.

Emergency Funds

The Academy of American Poets
584 Broadway, Suite 1208, New York, NY 10012-3250
Phone: 212-274-0343   Email: academy@dti.net
Fax: 212-274-9427   Website: www.poets.org

Services: The American Poets Fund provides confidential assistance to poets in the event of illness or other emergency.

Artists' Fellowships, Inc.
c/o The Salmagundi Club, 47 Fifth Ave., New York, NY 10003
Phone: 212-255-7740

Services: Offers financial aid to professional artists in time of need. Letters of request are reviewed monthly.

Art Matters
See page 72.

Blues Heaven
2120 Michigan Ave. S, Chicago, IL 60616
Phone: 312-808-1286
Website: www.mercenary.com/cgi-local/shop.pl/page=blues_heaven.html

Services: The Emergency Assistance Resolve was established to help blues musicians, with or without insurance, to receive medical treatments.

Grants, Funds & Employment - Emergency Funds

Chicago Artists' Coalition (CAC)

11 Hubbard St. E, Seventh Fl., Chicago, IL 60611
Phone: 312-670-2060   Website: www.caconline.org
Fax: 312-670-2521

Services: The CAC is an artist-run coalition of visual artists who strive to educate, advocate, provide services, and improve the environment in which artists live. Members of the Coalition have access to group health insurance, short-term dental, disability, and life insurance. A monthly newspaper, slide registry, job referral service, emergency fund, free lectures, workshops, and numerous publications are also offered to those who join. CAC hosts regular workshops, lectures, and panel discussions on topics of immediate interest to artists.

Fees: $25/students, $30/seniors, $40/regular annual membership.

Craft Emergency Relief Fund (CERF)

PO Box 838, Montpelier, VT 05601-0838
Phone: 802-229-2306   Email: info@craftemergency.org
Fax: 802-223-6484   Website: www.craftemergency.org

Services: The Craft Emergency Relief Fund (CERF) is a nonprofit organization which provides immediate support to professional craftspeople facing career threatening emergencies such as fire, theft, illness, and natural disaster.

CreArte

See page 22.

Every Penny Counts

PO Box 582943, Minneapolis, MN 55458-2943
Phone: 612-331-7733

Services: Provides emergency financial assistance to low income people with AIDS and HIV. The fund is separated into The AIDS Emergency Fund for people diagnosed with AIDS, and The Care Emergency Fund for people with HIV.

Grants, Funds & Employment - Emergency Funds

Adolph and Esther Gottlieb Foundation, Inc.

380 W Broadway, New York, NY 10012-5115

Phone: 212-226-0581

Fax: 212-226-0584

Services: The Foundation provides ten individual support grants to painters, sculptors, and printmakers who have been working for a minimum of 20 years in a mature phase of their art and have financial need. They also administer an emergency assistance program year-round, which assists artists suffering from recent catastrophic circumstances, who have worked for a minimum of ten years in a mature phase of their art.

Lotta Theatrical Fund

11 Beacon St., Suite 1110, Boston, MA 02108

Phone: 617-742-5920

Services: Grants starting at $50 are available to both men and women in the theatrical field for use in an emergency. Scholarships are also given to young female dramatists.

The Minneapolis Foundation

A200 Foshay Tower, 821 Marquette Ave. S, Minneapolis, MN 55402

Phone: 612-339-7343

Fax: 612-672-3846

Services: The Fund provides money (up to $700) to families in the west metro area in the cases of unforeseen emergency situations, specifically housing emergencies. Grants are not given directly to individuals, but to qualified organizations who serve as a liaison.

Grants, Funds & Employment - Emergency Funds/Employment

MusiCares Foundation
3402 Pico Blvd., Santa Monica, CA 90405
Toll-Free: 800-687-4227
Website: www.grammy.com/musicares/index.html

Services: MusiCares provides a life-line to music people in need of financial or other assistance. MusiCares programs are self-supported through fundraising activities, including such long-term goals as the creation of health clinics and retirement facilities for the music community.

P.E.N. Writers Fund
See page 68.

Ramsey Action Programs for Washington County
1397 Geneva Ave. N, Suite 103, Oakdale, MN 55128
Phone: 651-738-1910   Email: mcarroll@ramseyactionprograms.org
Fax: 651-788-7084

Services: Emergency grants and loans are available to persons who do not qualify for other forms of assistance. Loans are available for emergency rent or mortgage assistance and self-sufficiency (employment related). Short term loans are available for childcare and to college students, depending on funding available.

Employment

ArtJob Online
Western State Arts Federation, 1543 Champa St., Suite 220, Denver, CO 80202
Phone: 303-629-1166   Email: staff@westaf.org
Fax: 303-629-9717   Websites: www.westaf.org
Toll-Free: 888-562-7232   or: www.artjob.org
TTY: 303-607-9019   or: www.artistsregister.org

Services: ArtJob is an online resource for employment and opportunities in

ArtJob Online, cont.

the arts throughout the United States. The searchable website includes full- and part-time positions, internships, grants, fellowships, and calls for entries. Job seekers also have access to an employer database that includes background and contact information about employers in the arts.

Aviso
American Association of Museums
1125 Eye St. NW, Suite 200, Washington, DC 20005
Phone: 202-289-1818   Email: aviso@aam-us.org
Fax: 202-789-1355   Website: www.aam-us.org/adviso/

Services: *Aviso* is a monthly newsletter that provides up-to-date information about the museum field, as well as listings on employment, goods, and services for the museum professional.

Chicago Artists' Coalition (CAC)
See page 84.

Hennepin County Human Resources Department
A-400 Hennepin Co. Govt. Ctr., 300 Sixth St. S, Minneapolis, MN 55487-0040
Phone: 612-348-2163   Website: www.co.hennepin.mn.us
Fax: 612-348-6224
TTY: 612-348-5016

Services: Lists employment opportunities in Hennepin County.

Resources and Counseling for the Arts
308 Prince St., Suite 270, St. Paul, MN 55102
Phone: 651-292-4381   Email: info@rc4arts.org
Fax: 651-292-4315   Website: www.rc4arts.org
TTY: 651-292-3218

Services: RCA maintains job listings for people interested in a career in the arts. Listings are broken down into local and national "Job Books" which

Grants, Funds & Employment - Employment

Resources and Counseling for the Arts, cont.

may be perused at no charge at RCA's website or at the Resources and Counseling office. Listings are updated weekly. Career consultations are available from RCA's staff.

Education: Workshops are conducted quarterly.

Fees: $30/hour for consultations. Workshop fees vary.

WomenVenture

Midtown Commons, 2324 University Ave., St. Paul, MN 55114

Phone: 651-646-3808

Fax: 651-641-7223

Services: WomenVenture provides individual career counseling, business counseling, assorted job listings, and other support services for women.

Education: Career planning, business development, and advancement classes on financing, planning, and more are held throughout the metro Twin Cities region.

Business & Legal Services

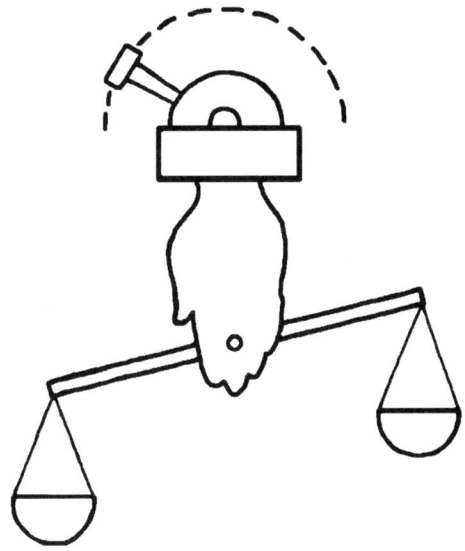

Credit Counseling	90
Financial Management	91
Accounting	93
Government Services	94
Copyright & Patent	95
Advocacy	95
Mediation	98
Legal Assistance	99

Credit Counseling

Consumer Credit Counseling Service

430 Oak Grove St., Minneapolis, MN 55403

Phone: 612-874-8164

Services: This nonprofit credit counseling service features a debt repayment program, and negotiates between debtors and creditors.

Fees: Sliding fee scale.

Family & Children's Service

414 Eighth St. S, Minneapolis, MN 55404

Phone: 612-339-9101 (Downtown office)

Services: Family and Children's Service offers a comprehensive range of services and initiatives to strengthen individuals, families, and communities. These include mental health counseling, credit counseling, family support services, family life education, policy and community initiatives, and school success programs.

Fees: Sliding scale based on ability to pay.

Lutheran Social Service of Minnesota - Credit Counseling Service

2485 Como Ave., St. Paul, MN 55108-1445

Phone: 651-642-5990   Website: www.lssmn.org/financial.htm

Fax: 651-969-2360

Toll-Free: 800-582-5260

Services: Counselors provide budget counseling, debt repayment services, and education to families and individuals who may be experiencing financial difficulty. LSS also provides housing counseling services to include prepurchasing a home, foreclosure, and home buyer workshops.

The Village Family Service Center
3400 First St. N, Suite 103, St. Cloud, MN 56303
Phone: 320-253-0541   Website: www.thevillagefamily.org
Fax: 320-253-0541
Toll-Free: 800-450-4019

Services: The Village is a nonprofit program that advises individuals, families, and groups on effective money management, offering workshops, budget and credit counseling, educational seminars, and private sessions on how to successfully finance living expenses.

Fees: $15 assessment fee.

Financial Management

The Artists' Tax Guide and Financial Planner
by Carla Messman, available at the Minneapolis Public Libraries
Phone: 612-630-6000   Website: www.mpls.lib.mn.us

Services: Includes sections on "The Artist as Business Owner" and "Special Tax Topics," both of which cover bookkeeping, recordkeeping, reporting, capitalization, depreciation, inventories, profits, audits, and much more.

Insurance Brokers of Minnesota
c/o Brian Netzer, 8032 Perry Ave. N, Brooklyn Park, MN 55443
Phone: 763-561-5510   Email: bdm004@underwriters.com
Fax: 763-560-6213

Services: Insurance Brokers of Minnesota provide studio insurance for artists.

MAP for Nonprofits
See page 4.

Business & Legal Services - Financial Management

Minnesota Department of Revenue

Phone: 651-296-3781   Website: www.taxes.state.mn.us
Toll-Free: 800-652-9094

Services: The Minnesota Department of Revenue website offers information on filing taxes, utilities payments, and current financial issues for individuals as well as businesses.

Fees: None.

John Munger

1451 Holton St., St. Paul, MN 55108
Phone: 651-646-8076   Email: jrmdance@aol.com
Fax: 651-646-7971

Services: Munger offers financial planning and management, as well as mid and long-range strategic planning for performing arts groups. Special expertise in dance.

Fees: $65/hour.

Resources and Counseling for the Arts

308 Prince St., Suite 270, St. Paul, MN 55101
Phone: 651-292-4381   Email: info@rc4arts.org
Fax: 651-292-4315   Website: www.rc4arts.org
TTY: 651-292-3218

Services: RCA offers workshops and individual consultations on starting a small business, nonprofit and for-profit options, taxes, recordkeeping, business development, and management topics. Some workshops and seminars are related to the Dayton Hudson Artists Loan Fund. RCA provides referrals to area accountants and attorneys who specialize in tax issues of artists and nonprofit cultural organizations.

Fees: Workshop fees vary. Call for consulting rates.

Tax Clinic

229 19th Ave. S, 190 Law Center, Minneapolis, MN 55455

Phone: 612-625-5515

Services: Clients are accepted on the basis of income for assistance with audits and tax or district courts.

Fees: Clients must pay their own filing fees, but the Clinic is free.

United Way First Call for Help – Minneapolis Branch

See page 82.

United Way First Call for Help – St. Paul Branch

See page 82.

The Village Family Service Center

See page 91.

Accounting

Resources and Counseling for the Arts

308 Prince St., Suite 270, St. Paul, MN 55101

Phone: 651-292-4381   Email: info@rc4arts.org

Fax: 651-292-4315   Website: www.rc4arts.org

TTY: 651-292-3218

Services: RCA has a comprehensive referral listing of accountants who are sensitive to the needs of the arts community.

Government Services

The Art Law Primer
by Linda Pinkerton and John Guardalabene, 31 21st St. W, New York, NY 10010
Phone: 212-620-9580

Services: This book contains chapters on copyrights, written agreements, artist/dealer relationships, reproductions and publications, leases, financial considerations, moral rights, U.S. customs and immigration, and legal aid.

Attorney General's Consumer Protection Division
1400 NCL Tower, 445 Minnesota St., St. Paul, MN 55101
Phone: 651-296-3353   Email: attorney.general@state.mn.us
Fax: 651-296-9963
Website: www.ag.state.mn.us/home/consumer/default.shtml
Toll-Free: 800-657-3787   TTY: 651-297-7206

Services: This organization mediates disputes between consumers and businesses, or refers them to other government agencies. Information is provided on consumer laws/issues via telephone and brochure.

City of Duluth
330 City Hall, 411 First St. W, Duluth, MN 55802
Phone: 218-723-3300   Email: webcomment@ci.duluth.mn.us
Websites: www.ci.duluth.mn.us/city/economic/ (general)
   or: www.dpac@ci.duluth.mn.us (Public Arts Commission)

City of Minneapolis
City Hall, 350 Fifth St. S, Minneapolis, MN 55415
Phone: 612-673-3000   Website: www.ci.mpls.mn.us/index.html
TTY: (612) 673-2157

City of Rochester
201 Fourth St. SE, Rochester, MN 55904
Phone: 507-285-8086 Email: cityhall@ci.rochester.mn.us
Fax: 507-285-8256 Website: www.ci.rochester.mn.us

City of St. Paul
City Hall, 15 Kellogg Blvd. W, St. Paul, MN 55102
Phone: 651-266-8989 Website: www.stpaul.gov

Minnesota Department of Revenue
See page 92.

Minnesota Department of Transportation
Transportation Building, 395 John Ireland Blvd., St. Paul, MN 55155
Phone: 651-296-2385 Email: info@dot.state.mn.us
Toll-Free: 800-657-3774 Website: www.dot.state.mn.us
TTY: 651-296-9930

Services: The Minnesota DOT provides road, public transportation, and travel information.

Copyright & Patent

The Art Law Primer
See page 94.

Business & Legal Services - Copyright & Patent/Advocacy

United States Copyright Office
The Library of Congress
101 Independence Ave. SE, Washington, DC 20559-6000
Phone: 202-707-3000 (info)   Email: copyinfo@loc.gov
       or: 202-707-9100 (to order forms)   Website: www.loc.gov/copyright
Fax: 202-707-2600

Services: The US Copyright Office is established to promote the progress of science and useful arts by securing to authors and inventors (for limited times) the exclusive right to their respective writings and discoveries.

United States Patent & Trademark Office
Box OED, Washington, DC 20231
Phone: 703-308-4357   Website: www.uspto.gov
Toll-Free: 800-786-9199

Services: The United States Patent and Trademark Office website and hotline provides information on rights and legal issues surrounding copyright, patent, and trademarking.

Advocacy

Actors' Equity Association Hotline
See page 61.

American Arts Alliance
805 15th St. NW, Suite 500, Washington, DC 20005
Phone: 202-289-1776   Email: aaa@artswire.org
Fax: 203-371-6601   Website: www.artswire.org/~aaa/

Services: The American Arts Alliance is an advocate for America's nonprofit arts organizations and their publics in representing arts interests and advancing arts support before Congress and other branches of government.

Americans for the Arts

1000 Vermont Ave. NW, 12th Fl., Washington, DC 20005
Phone: 202-371-2830 Website: www.artsusa.org/advocacy/
Fax: 202-371-0424

Services: Americans for the Arts works with cultural organizations, arts and business leaders, and individuals to provide leadership, education, and information that will encourage support for the arts and culture in our nation's communities.

Fees: Varying levels of membership available.

Minnesota Alliance for Arts in Education

See page 28.

Minnesota Citizens for the Arts

708 First St. N, Suite 235D, Minneapolis, MN 55401-1145
Phone: 612-338-2970 Email: mca@mtn.org
Fax: 612-338-2907 Website: www.mtn.org/mca

Services: Minnesota Citizens for the Arts (MCA) is a statewide nonprofit arts advocacy organization whose mission is to provide access to the arts for all Minnesotans. MCA organizes the arts community and lobbies the Minnesota State Legislature and Congress on issues pertaining to the nonprofit arts community.

Education: MCA's advocacy seminars teach people how their government works encourages involvement.

National Artists Equity Association

PO Box 28068, Central Station, Washington, DC 20038
Phone: 202-628-9633
Toll-Free: 800-727-NAEA

Services: In addition to assisting with advocacy, information, and education, the National Artists Equity Association offers health and art insurance to members.

Fees: $40 annual membership, and insurance costs are additional.

Business & Legal Services - Advocacy/Mediation

National Association for the Self-Employed
See page 8

New York Artist Equity Association (NYAEA)
498 Broome St., New York, NY 10013
Phone: 212-941-0130   Email: reginas@anny.org
Fax: 212-941-0138   Website: www.anny.org

Services: The New York Artist Equity Association is a politically non-partisan nonprofit resource network and service organization to the visual arts. Its primary purpose is to disseminate information regarding legislation and legal rights, all in the interest of effectively addressing "survival" issues specifically relevant to artists.

Twin Cities Musicians Union – Local 30-73
See page 60.

Mediation

Attorney General's Consumer Protection Division
See page 94.

Dispute Resolution Center
974 Seventh St. W, St. Paul, MN 55102
Phone: 651-292-7791   Email: drc@spacestar.net
Fax: 651-292-6065

Services: Mediation for problems involving neighbors, family, landlord/tenants, business/consumers, borrowers/lenders, employer/employees, post-divorce, and visitation issues. Referrals are also available.

Fees: $25/party for a two hour session. Fees may be waived for lower-income clients.

Legal Assistance

Graphic Artists Guild
See page 42.

Legal Aid Society of Minnesota
430 First Ave. N, Minneapolis, MN 55401
Phone: 612-332-1441

Services: Legal Aid Society provides family law, divorces, government benefits, and housing law for clients below the poverty line. They also have a Disability Law Center.

Fees: Based on ability to pay. Free services to those who are income eligible.

Minnesota State Bar Association Attorney Referral Service
600 Nicollet Ave., Suite 380, Minneapolis, MN 55402
Toll-Free: 800-292-4152   Website: www.mnbar.org/attref.htm

Services: The Minnesota State Bar Association can help match clients with an attorney, provides listings of other Minnesota Referral Services, as well as tips on how to handle specific legal issues.

New York Artists Equity Association, Inc.
See page 98.

Resources and Counseling for the Arts
308 Prince St., Suite 270, St. Paul, MN 55101
Phone: 651-292-4381   Email: info@rc4arts.org
Fax: 651-292-4315   Website: www.rc4arts.org
TTY: 651-292-3218

Services: RCA maintains an attorney referral file for artists and small arts organizations.

Fees: Telephone consultations with participating attorneys are free up to a half-hour. Artists who go on to work with particular attorneys generally do so at a negotiated reduced fee.

Business & Legal Services - Legal Assistance

Volunteer Lawyer's Network

514 Nicollet Mall, Suite 350A, Minneapolis, MN 55402
Phone: 612-339-9139 (info);
or: 612-339-5500 (administration)

Services: The Volunteer Lawyer's Network provides free legal services to Hennepin County clients below the poverty line. No suing or fee generating work is accepted.

Health & Human Services

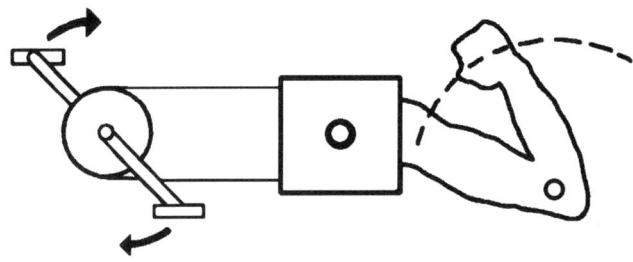

Housing & Studio Space	101
Health Insurance	102
Sliding Scale Medical	106
AIDS Info and Services	110
Occupational Health & Safety	111
Alternative Forms of Healthcare	112
Utilities Assistance	113
Crisis Intervention	114
Food	117
Disability Services	118
Childcare	120

Health & Human Services - Housing & Studio Space

Housing & Studio Space

Artspace Projects, Inc.

528 Hennepin Ave. S, Suite 404, Minneapolis, MN 55403

Phone: 612-333-9012   Email: Artspace@artspaceprojects.org

Fax: 612-333-9089   Website: www.artspaceprojects.org

Services: Artspace is a developer of spaces for studio, performance, rehearsal, exhibition, and living uses for artists in all genres. They also have a space referral/resource program which assists in locating spaces throughout the Twin Cities.

Minneapolis Community Development Agency

See page 79.

Minneapolis Tenant's Union

610 28th St. W, Minneapolis, MN 55408

Phone: 612-871-7485

Services: This number lists the times during the week when the Union is open for walk-in consultation. They also have a paid hotline service number which is accessible through the main line.

Minnesota Housing Finance Agency

See page 81.

Neighborhood Revitalization Program

Crown Roller Mill, Suite 425, 105 Fifth Ave. S, Minneapolis, MN 55401

Phone: 612-673-5140   Email: internet@nrp.org

Fax: 612-673-5138   Website: www.nrp.org

Services: The Minneapolis Neighborhood Revitalization Program is an effort to bring residents into the priority-setting process of their city. NRP funds function as "start-up" money for the revitalization of neighborhoods.

St. Paul Housing Information Office

25 Fourth St. W, St. Paul, MN 55102

Phone: 651-266-6000   Website: www.stpaul.gov/depts

Services: The Office provides all types of housing information and referrals to other agencies on a phone or walk-in basis. Although their main focus is on the St. Paul vicinity, the Office also has information on Ramsey and Anoka counties.

St. Paul Planning and Economic Development

See page 79.

Twin Cities Neighborhood Housing

Exchange Building, 26 Exchange St. E, St. Paul, MN 55101

Phone: 651-297-6227

Services: The Neighborhood Housing office is the central referral for four groups: the Southside Minneapolis Neighborhood Housing Service, the Westside St. Paul Neighborhood Housing Service, the Northside Minneapolis Neighborhood Housing Service, and the Dayton's Bluff Neighborhood Housing Service. These are all planning and development groups for the respective neighborhoods.

Health Insurance

The Actors' Fund of America

729 Seventh Ave., Tenth Fl., New York, NY 10019

Phone: 212-221-7300   Email: jbrown@actorsfund.org

Fax: 212-764-0238   Website: www.actorsfund.org/ahirc

Toll-Free: 800-798-8447

Services: The Actors' Fund is established to provide for the social welfare of all entertainment professionals in times of need. Through the Artists' Health Insurance Resource Center, The Actors' Fund provides the arts community with information on a community and national basis to inform artists of their health insurance options.

Health & Human Services - Health Insurance

American Institute of Graphic Arts
See page 40.

American Society of Media Photographers
See page 45.

Chicago Artists' Coalition (CAC)
See page 84.

College Art Association
See page 3.

The Dramatists Guild of America
See page 61.

Graphic Artists Guild
See page 42.

Health Insurance: A Guide for Artists, Consultants, Entrepreneurs and Other Self-Employed
by Lenore Janecek, published by the American Council for the Arts
Dept. 32, 1 E 53rd St., New York, NY 10022
Phone: 212-223-ARTS
Toll-Free: 800-321-4510

Services: *Health Insurance* recommends ways to get the most out of health benefits, tips on how to find the right doctor, approaches to avoiding health problems that affect artists, and a list of insurance resources for artists.

International Documentary Association
See page 44.

International Sculpture Center
See page 37.

MinnesotaCare
Minnesota Dept. of Human Services, 444 Lafayette Rd. N, St. Paul, MN 55155
Phone: 651-297-3862
Toll-Free: 800-657-3672
Website: www.dhs.state.mn.us/hlthcare/asstprog/mncare/default.htm

Services: MinnesotaCare is a health care plan available to Minnesotans who do not have health insurance. Coverage includes most medical, dental, and preventative care, with no exclusions for pre-existing conditions.

Fees: A sliding scale fee is available under the current plan.

Minnesota Comprehensive Health Association
PO Box 64566, St. Paul, MN 55164
Phone: 651-662-5290   Email: mchaminn@aol.com
Toll-Free: 800-531-6674   Website: www.mchamn.com

Services: Minnesota Comprehensive offers policies of individual health insurance to those considered "uninsurable" due to pre-existing conditions, line of work, high risk, etc.

National Artists Equity Association
See page 97.

National Sculpture Society
See page 37.

National Writers Union
See page 67.

Percussive Arts Society, Minnesota Chapter
See page 59.

Health & Human Services - Health Insurance/Sliding Scale Medical

Twin Cities Musicians Union
See page 60.

Women's Caucus for Art – National Office
PO Box 1498, Canal St. Station, New York, NY 10013
Phone: 212-634-0007   Email: info@nationalwca.com
Website: nationalwca.com

Services: Membership open to women and men artists, arts administrators, teachers, students, and curators. Offers major medical, short-term medical, life, and disability through Wohlers Insurance Company.

Sliding Scale Medical

Community-University Health Care Center
2001 Bloomington Ave. S, Minneapolis, MN 55404
Phone: 612-627-4774 or 612-627-4205 (Administration)
   or: 612-627-4442 (Medical clinic)

Services: Medical, dental, and mental health services are offered. The Center has a prepay program which covers certain services provided at the Fairview University Medical Center.

Family Medical Center
5 Lake St. W, Minneapolis, MN 55408
Phone: 612-827-9800
Fax: 612-827-9874

Services: This family practice clinic provides exams, lab tests, prescriptions, and more for clients whose income is within 200% of the federal poverty guidelines. They specialize in sports medicine as well.

Fees: A part-pay program ranges according to income, and includes all services at the center.

Helping Hand Dental Clinic

506 Seventh St. W, St. Paul, MN 55102

Phone: 651-224-7561   Toll-Free: 800-942-7858

Services: The Clinic accepts local residents who are on medical assistance as well as privately insured clients.

Fees: Sliding fee scale according to income.

Hennepin County Assured Care Program

525 Portland Ave., Third Fl., Minneapolis, MN 55415

Phone: 612-348-6141

Services: Assured Care is a discounted, sliding fee scale system for all services offered by Hennepin County, including emergency room services. The application procedure is free, available to anyone, and membership is renewable annually.

Indian Health Board

1315 24th St. E, Minneapolis, MN 55404

Phone: 612-721-9800

Services: The Health Board provides medical care, dental care, and counseling support, as well as outreach programs for prenatal care, diabetics, and people trying to quit smoking. Services are available to anyone, not only Native Americans.

Fees: Sliding fee scale according to income.

Medical Assistance – Hennepin County

330 11th St. S, Minneapolis, MN 55404

Phone: 612-348-2722

Services: Medical Assistance is the state-sponsored health program for low-income people and single adults. Applications are taken in person only.

Health & Human Services - Sliding Scale Medical

Medical Assistance – Ramsey County

160 Kellogg Blvd. E, St. Paul, MN 55101-1494
Phone: 651-266-4444   Email: Laurie.Encinas@Co.Ramsey.mn.us
Fax: 651-266-3709 attn: Laurie

Services: Provide federal and state-sponsored health programs for people with low income.

Minneapolis Department of Health and Family Support

250 Fourth St. S, Suite 510, Minneapolis, MN 55415-1372
Phone: 612-673-2301   Website: www.ci.minneapolis.mn.us.dhfs
Fax: 612-673-3866

Services: The Department of Health and Family Support offers laboratory services, employment and training programs, public health research and policy development, housing advocacy, American Indian advocacy, and senior citizen services.

Fees: Most services are free or on a sliding fee scale.

Neighborhood Health Care Network

2550 University Ave. W, Suite 416 S, St. Paul, MN 55114
Phone: 651-489-2273   Email: info@nchn.org
Fax: 651-649-0725

Services: Neighborhood Health Care Network is an alliance of community clinics in the Twin Cities and surrounding areas. Network members provide a wide range of services including primary, prenatal, reproductive, and dental care.

Planned Parenthood of Minnesota

1965 Ford Pkwy., St. Paul, MN 55116
Phone: 651-698-2406

Services: Planned Parenthood offers women's health care and counseling at five clinics in the Twin Cities metro area.

Fees: Based on client's ability to pay.

Health & Human Services - Sliding Scale Medical

Sage Women's Clinic

118 W Market, Mall of America, Bloomington, MN 55425
Phone: 612-676-5001 (Appointments), or: 612-883-0440 (Clinic)
Fax: 612-883-0456

Services: Free mammograms and PAPS offered to women over 40 who meet income guidelines and who have no health insurance or have insurance but have an unmet deductible or co-pay.

University of Minnesota School of Dentistry

Malcom Moos Health Science Tower, 515 Delaware St. SE, Minneapolis, MN 55455
Phone: 612-625-0986

Services: The U of M Dentistry School offers dental services for clients of all ages, including limited, uncomplicated oral surgery. Services are by appointment only.

Fees: Reduced rate.

Women's and Children's Health Programs

6601 Shingle Creek Pkwy., Brooklyn Center, MN 55430
Phone: 612-569-2660 (General), or: 612-569-2670 (Women's Health Line)
   or: 612-569-2680 (Children's Health Line)

Services: Women's health care includes pregnancy testing, family planning, Pap and pelvic exams, prenatal care and delivery, nutrition and health information, and referrals. Clinics are located in Hopkins, Bloomington, and Brooklyn Center. Children's health care includes pediatric exams, referrals; developmental, vision, hearing, and speech screenings; immunizations, dental care referrals, and counseling for parents.

Fees: Sliding scale fees based on income and family size.

AIDS Info & Services

Aliveness Project

730 38th St. E, Minneapolis, MN 55407

Phone: 612-822-7946 Email: STAFF@aliveness.org
Fax: 612-822-9668 Website: www.aliveness.org

Services: The Project offers food and clothing shelves, a massage and chiropractic clinic, and support groups at their center for persons living with AIDS or who are HIV+.

Art Matters

See page 72.

Every Penny Counts

See page 84.

Minnesota AIDS Project

1400 Park Ave. S, Minneapolis, MN 55404

Phone: 612-341-2060 Website: www.mnaidsproject.org
or: 612-373-2437 (MAP AIDSline)
Fax: 612-341-4057
Toll-Free: 800-248-AIDS

Services: Through MAP's offices in Minneapolis and throughout the state, Minnesotans living with HIV and AIDS are provided confidential services, including practical, emotional, and social support. MAP staff and volunteers also provide HIV and AIDS education through the AIDSline, Speakers' Bureau, Outreach, and County and State Fairs. The MAP AIDSline acts as the entry point for questions about HIV/AIDS, services, or support needs throughout the State of Minnesota.

P.E.N. Fund for Writers and Editors with HIV/AIDS

See page 76.

Occupational Health & Safety

American Alliance for Health, Physical Education, Recreation and Dance
1900 Association Dr., Reston, VA 20191
Phone: 703-476-3400 Email: webmaster@aahperd.org
Toll-Free: 800-213-7193 Website: www.aahperd.org

Services: The American Alliance for Health, Physical Education, Recreation and Dance (AAHPERD) is the largest organization of professionals supporting and assisting those involved in physical education, leisure, fitness, dance, health promotion, and education and all specialties related to achieving a healthy lifestyle.

Center for Safety in the Arts
Email: csa@artswire.org Website: www.artswire.org:70/1/csa

Services: The Center's website provides information on hazards in the visual arts, performing arts, children and school arts programs, museums, and general health and safety information and laws relevant to the arts. The information is primarily intended for artists, performers and others working in the arts, and most of the files are written for people without a health and safety background.

Occupational Health Services
St. Paul – Ramsey Medical Center, 640 Jackson St., St. Paul, MN 55101
Phone: 651-221-3313

Services: Provides rehabilitation services for people injured or disabled so that they are able to return to work and their normal way of living.

Health & Human Services - Alternative Forms of Healthcare

Alternative Forms of Healthcare

American Music Therapy Association, Inc. (AMTA)
See page 55.

Arts and Healing Network
Website: www.artheals.org

Services: The Arts and Healing Network is a web site resource for anyone interested in the healing potential of art, especially environmentalists, social activists, artists, health care practitioners, and those challenged by illness. The site features an extensive section on community-based projects, the work of over 200 visual artists, and an interactive bulletin board. In addition the site includes a resource section of books, grants, artist resources, and more.

Fairview Arts Medical Center
825 Nicollet Mall, 507 Medical Arts Building, Minneapolis, MN 55402
Phone: 612-332-ARTS   Toll-Free: 888-750-ARTS

Services: The Center is dedicated to meeting the distinctive healthcare needs of artists and arts educators.

Minnesota Art Therapy Association
See page 8.

Minnesota Association for Music Therapy
See page 57.

Minnesota Therapeutic Massage Network
3010 Hennepin Ave. S, Minneapolis, MN 55408
Phone: 612-879-4337

Services: The Network is mostly a resource for massage practitioners and their issues, but also is a referral resource for finding practitioners.

National Association for Poetry Therapy (NAPT)
See page 67.

Pathways
3115 Hennepin Ave. S, Minneapolis, MN 55408
Phone: 612-822-9061　　　　Email: pathways@mtn.org
Fax: 612-822-9061　　　　　Website: www.pathwaysminneapolis.org

Services: Pathways has programs in bodywork, massage, spirituality, and psychological support groups for persons who have a life-threatening illness or are healing.
Fees: Free.

Utilities Assistance

Center for Energy and Environment
100 Sixth St. N, Suite 412A, Minneapolis, MN 55403
Phone: 612-335-5858

Services: The Center offers energy audits and consulting services for homeowners and small business owners, primarily in lower-income brackets.

Energy Assistance Program
PO Box 678, Hopkins, MN 55343
Phone: 952-930-3373
or: 952-930-3541 (Screening Line)

Services: The Energy Assistance Program assists low income-individuals with their energy bills.

Minnesota Public Utilities Commission
121 Seventh Pl. E, Suite 350, St. Paul, MN 55101
Phone: 651-296-7124

Services: The Commission administers Link Up Minnesota, which assists individuals who have a low household income with up to half their telephone installation and connection charges.

Health & Human Services - Utilities Assistance/Crisis Intervention

Ramsey Action Programs, Inc.
450 Syndicate St. N, St. Paul, MN 55104
Phone: 651-645-6470

Services: Ramsey Action Programs offers a number of useful informational and assistance programs including an energy assistance program to help renters and homeowners pay utility and fuel bills during winter months.
Fees: Sliding fee scale.

Salvation Army Heat/Share – Minneapolis
1841 Lake St. E, Minneapolis, MN 55407
Phone: 612-721-1668

Services: Minneapolis residents with low and moderate income may be eligible for emergency funds for furnace repair or payment of energy bills.

Salvation Army Heat/Share – Ramsey County
401 Seventh St. W, St. Paul, MN 55102
Phone: 651-870-0529

Services: Residents of the St. Paul/Ramsey County area may be eligible for emergency funds to repair furnaces or pay energy bills.

Crisis Intervention

Chrysalis Center for Women
2650 Nicollet Ave. S, Minneapolis, MN 55408
Phone: 612-871-0118   Email: info@chrysaliswomen.org
Fax: 612-871-1814   Website: www.chrysaliswomen.org
TTY: 612-871-3652

Services: This organization assists women and families who find themselves in crisis or transition, providing telephone counseling, support groups, legal services, mental health services, and chemical dependency services.

Health & Human Services - Crisis Intervention

Crisis Connection

PO Box 19550, Minneapolis, MN 55419
Crisis Helpline: 612-379-6363
Phone: 612-379-6388 (Admin.)   Email: office@crisis.org
Fax: 612-379-6391   Website: www.crisis.org
TTY: 612-379-6397
Services: Call for mental health counseling, emergencies, and referrals.
Fees: None.

Greater Minneapolis Crisis Nursery

5400 Glenwood Ave., Golden Valley, MN 55422
Crisis Line: 763-591-0100
Phone: 763-591-0400 (Admin.)   Email: info@mail.crisisnursery.org
Fax: 763-591-0700   Website: www.crisisnursery.org
Services: The Greater Minneapolis Crisis Nursery works in partnership with parents in crisis and the community to strengthen families and prevent child abuse and neglect. Their services include care for children for up to three days, 24-hour/7-day crisis hotline, information and referrals, parent support groups, in-home visits, emergency short-term daycare, and advocacy.

Hennepin County Child Protection Hotline

24 hour hotline: 612-348-3552
Services: The Child Protection Hotline responds to reports of child abuse and neglect.

Minneapolis Handbook of the Streets

Alliance of the Streets, 1321 First Ave. S, Minneapolis, MN 55403
Phone: 612-870-0529
Services: A guide to food shelves, free clothing, meals, shelters, health care, and legal services for those in need.
Fees: No charge for handbook.

Health & Human Services - Crisis Intervention

Musician's Assistance Program
See page 59.

Outfront Minnesota
310 38th St. E, Suite 204, Minneapolis, MN 55409-1300
Phone: 612-822-0127   Toll-Free: 800-800-0350

Services: Outfront Minnesota offers same-sex domestic violence intervention, anti-violence program including GLBT hate crimes reporting, and crime victim advocacy.

Sexual Offense Services of Ramsey County
1619 Dayton Ave, Suite 201, St. Paul, MN 55104
24-hour Crisis Line: 651-643-3006
Phone: 651-643-3022 (Admin.)
Email: sexual.offense.services@co.ramsey.mn.us
Fax: 651-643-3031
TTY: 651-643-3022

Services: SOS is the sexual violence victim crisis center for Ramsey County. It offers a 24-hour free and confidential hotline, short-term support and counseling, advocacy, outreach, crisis intervention, community education, and training.
Fees: None.

United Way First Call for Help – Minneapolis Branch
See page 82.

United Way First Call for Help – St. Paul Branch
See page 82.

Food

Emergency Foodshelf Network

6714 Walker St., Minneapolis, MN 55426

Phone: 612-925-6265

Services: The Emergency Foodshelf Network is the central organization of 27 foodshelves in Hennepin County. Call the Network regarding where to go for low cost quality food in the area.

Fare For All

729 Kasota Ave., Minneapolis, MN 55414

Phone: 612-331-6870   Toll-Free: 800-582-4291

Fax: 612-331-6873

Services: Fare For All is dedicated to providing quality food to all interested families and individuals at an affordable price. At the same time, they encourage volunteer service to build strong communities. Food is pre-ordered and pre-paid. Distribution is one day per month.

Fees: $15 and applicable transportation fees; accepts cash, food stamps, EBS.

Second Harvest St. Paul Food Bank

1140 Gervais Ave., St. Paul, MN 55109-2042

Phone: 651-484-5117

Fax: 651-484-1064

Services: Second Harvest's programs include Twelve Baskets, a prepared and perishable food rescue program which delivers unused portions of food to hungry people; The Produce Program, where member agencies are able to receive fresh produce and distribute it to their clients; Mothers and Children/Nutrition Assistance Program for Seniors; and The Product Recovery Center which processes damaged but usable products recovered from SuperValu stores.

Disability Services

ADA Minnesota – Metropolitan Center for Independent Living
1600 University Ave. W, Suite 16, St. Paul, MN 55104-3825
Phone: 651-603-2015   Toll-Free: 888-845-4595
Fax: 651-603-2006

Services: ADA Minnesota provides information, technical assistance, and training to businesses, nonprofits, and people with disabilities (as it relates to the Americans for Disabilities Act).

Descriptive Video Service
Phone: 617-300-3490 (General)   Email: dvs@wgbh.org
   or: 888-818-1181 (Braille Guide/Catalog)
   or: 888-818-1999 (Large Print Guide/Catalog)
Fax: 617-300-3466   Website: www.wgbh.org/dvs
Toll-Free: 800-333-1203

Services: Applies the art of describing visual images for TV, home video, and film for people who are blind or visually impaired. A stereo television *or* a stereo VCR with the SAP feature required to access DVS on television. Only a standard VCR required for DVS home videos.

Discapacitados Abriendose Caminos
608 Smith Ave. S, St. Paul, MN 55107
Phone: 651-293-1748
Fax: 651-293-1744

Services: A nonprofit agency that provides support and services to Latino families and their children with disabilities.
Fees: No fees for services.

Health & Human Services - Disability Services

Freedom of Speech

2344 Nicollet Ave. S, Suite 400, Minneapolis, MN 55404

Phone: 612-544-333   Email: fos@freedomofspeech.com

Fax: 612-872-7374   Website: www.freedomofspeech.com

Toll-Free: 877-FOS-4ACT

Services: Freedom of Speech offers a comprehensive line of Assistive Computer Technologies for people with visual, mobile, learning and sensory disabilities. Products include screen readers, scan and read, Braille displays/translators/embossers, personal data assistants, speech recognition, and language processing tools.

Education: Please call.

Fees: Please call.

Interact Center for the Visual and Performing Arts

212 Third Ave. N, Suite 140, Minneapolis, MN 55401

Phone: 612-339-5145   Email: icvpa1@aol.com

Fax: 612-339-7762

Services: Interact is a visual and performing art center for individuals with disabilities. The Center runs an on-sight gallery, and produces four gallery shows and two theater performances annually.

Minnesota State Services for the Blind

2200 University Ave. W, Suite 240, St. Paul, MN 55114

Phone: 651-642-0852

Fax: 651-649-5927

Services: The Communication Center's Braille section provides Braille formatting for the print-disabled. An electronic hook-up service is available for the fastest turnaround of Brailled information. They also produce audio tape transcriptions of written materials for a fee.

Fees: $0.70 per Braille page.

Health & Human Services - Disability Services/Childcare

VSA Arts of Minnesota

528 Hennepin Ave., Suite 305, Minneapolis, MN 55403
Phone: 612-332-3888   Email: mn@vsarts.org
Fax: 612-305-0132   Website: www.vsarts.org
Toll-Free: 800-801-3883
TTY: 612-332-3888

Services: VSA Arts is an international organization that creates learning opportunities through the arts for people with disabilities. The organization offers arts-based programs in creative writing, dance, drama, music, and visual arts.

Childcare

Children's Home Society of Minnesota

2230 Como Ave., St. Paul, MN 55108
Phone: 651-646-6393   Email: chsm@winternet.com
Fax: 651-646-0436

Services: Offers childcare, pregnancy counseling services, crisis nursery programs, foster homes, adoption, and post-adoption services.

Early Childhood Resource Center

1600 Lake St. E, Minneapolis, MN 55407
Phone: 612-721-0265   Website: www.ecrc1.org
Fax: 612-721-0435

Services: Early Childhood Resource Center is a nonprofit organization that assists communities by providing services which strengthen families and ensure the healthy development of children. They provide resource and referral information to parents and providers within South Minneapolis and surrounding communities.

Health & Human Services - Childcare

Greater Minneapolis Day Care Association

1628 Elliot Ave. S, Minneapolis, MN 55404

Phone: 612-341-1177 (General)
or: 612-341-2066 (Referral Service),
or: 612-341-0737 (Fee Subsidy Service)

Services: Offers childcare referral and fee subsidy services for parents, training for childcare providers, and employer services.

Hennepin County Children and Family Services Department

525 Portland Ave. S, Minneapolis, MN 55415

Phone: 612-348-2324   TTY: 612-348-3124

Fax: 612-348-6900

Services: Offers child protection, social services to adolescent parents, outpatient mental health services for children, subsidized daycare service, and after hours emergency social services. Both English and Spanish spoken.

Minnesota Childcare Resource and Referral Network

220 Robert St. S, St. Paul, MN 55107

Phone: 651-290-9704

Services: The Childcare Resource and Referral Network is a statewide information and referral service for all types of licensed childcare. Network offices offer daycare training and act as a link between people seeking childcare and childcare providers.

Fees: Sliding fee scale.

Index

A

Academy for Film and Television	43
Academy of American Poets, The	83
Actors' Equity Association Hotline	61, 96
Actors' Fund of America, The	103
ADA Minnesota - Metropolitan Center for Independent Living	118
Aliveness Project	110
American Alliance for Health, Physical Education, Recreation and Dance	111
American Arts Alliance	96
American Association of Museums/ Aviso	7
American Composers Forum	55, 72
American Council for the Arts Book Catalog	2
American Craft Council	48
American Dance Therapy Association, MN Chapter	63
American Indian Resource and Referral Database	20
American Institute of Architects	40
American Institute of Graphic Arts	40, 104
American Institute of Graphic Arts - Minnesota Chapter	40
American Music Center	55
American Music Therapy Association, Inc. (AMTA)	55, 112
American Sewing Guild	50
American Society of Interior Designers, Minneapolis Chapter	41
American Society of Media Photographers - Minneapolis/St Paul Chapter	45, 104
American Swedish Institute, The	20
Americans for the Arts	97

A cont.

Anderson Center at Tower View, The	77
Arrowhead Regional Arts Council (Region 3)	12, 76
Art Calendar Magazine	33
Artists Del Norte	33
Artists of Minnesota	2
Artists' Fellowships, Inc.	83
Artists' Tax Guide and Financial Planner, The	91
ArtJob Online	86
Art Law Primer, The	94, 95
Art Matters	72, 83, 110
ArtNetwork	31
Art Scraps	33
Arts and Business Council Inc.	7, 31
Arts and Healing Network	112
Arts Midwest	2
Art Source	31
Artspace Projects, Inc.	102
Artward Bound/Summit Arts	26
Asian American Press	24
Asian American Renaissance	20
Associated Sewing	50
Association for the Advancement of Hmong Women in Minnesota	20
Association of Independent Video and Filmmakers (AIVF)	43
Attorney General's Consumer Protection Division	94, 98
Authors Guild	66
Aviso	87
Ax-man Surplus	33

B

Ballet Arts Minnesota	63
Banfill-Locke Center for the Arts	15
Black Storytellers Alliance	65
Blacklock Nature Sanctuary Artist Fellowship Program	72
Blues Heaven	83
Burnsville Area Society for the Arts (BASA)	16
Bush Artist Fellows Program	72

C

Caponi Art Park & Learning Center	26
Cartoon Connections	36
Cedar Cultural Center	21
Center for Arts Criticism	26
Center for Asians and Pacific Islanders	21
Center for Energy and Environment	113
Center for Safety in the Arts	111
Central Minnesota Arts Board (Region 7W)	14, 77
Centro Cultural Chicano	21
Chamber Music America	56
Chicago Artists' Coalition (CAC)	84, 87, 104
Chicano Latinos unidos en Servicios (CLUES)	22
Children's Book Illustrators Guild	41, 66
Children's Home Society of Minnesota	120
Chrysalis Center for Women	114
Circle, The	25
City of Duluth	94
City of Minneapolis	94
City of Rochester	95

C cont.

City of St. Paul	95
Colleagues of Calligraphy	69
College Art Association	3, 104
College of Visual Arts	27
Community-University Health Care Center	106
COMPAS	3, 27
Consumer Credit Counseling Service	90
Costume Guild of Minnesota	50
Craft Emergency Relief Fund (CERF)	84
CreArte	22, 84
Crisis Connection	115

D

Dakota County Center for the Arts and Humanities	16
Descriptive Video Service	118
Discapacitados Abriendose Caminos	118
Dispute Resolution Center	98
Dramatists Guild of America	61, 104

E

Early Childhood Resource Center	120
Early Music America	56
East Central Arts Council (Region 7E)	14, 77
East Side Arts Council	10
Edina Art Center	16
Elk River Area Arts Council	10

E cont.

Emergency Foodshelf Network	117
Energy Assistance Program	113
Ethnic Dance Theater	77
Every Penny Counts	84, 110
Exhibit: A Basic Guide to Gallery and Exhibition Spaces in Minnesota	34

F

Fairview Arts Medical Center	112
Family & Children's Service	90
Family Medical Center	106
Fare For All	117
Five Wings Arts Council (Region 5)	13, 77
FORECAST Public Artworks	30
Foundation Center	73
Foundation Center Cooperating Collection	73
Franconia Sculpture Park	37
Franklin ArtWorks	16
Freedom of Speech	119
Freelancers Group	41

G

Gold Book, The	3
Adolph and Esther Gottlieb Foundation, Inc.	85
Grants: A Basic Guide to Grants for Minnesota Artists	73
Graphic Artists Guild	42, 99, 104
Greater Minneapolis Crisis Nursery	115
Greater Minneapolis Day Care Association	121
Guild of Metalsmiths	38

H

Hand Papermaking, Inc.	69
Handweavers' Guild of America	50
Health Insurance: A Guide for Artists, Consultants, Entrepreneurs and Other Self-Employed	104
Helping Hand Dental Clinic	107
Hennepin County Assured Care Program	107
Hennepin County Child Protection Hotline	115
Hennepin County Children and Family Services Department	121
Hennepin County Human Resources Department	87
Hopkins Center for the Arts	17

I

Independent Feature Project/North	43
Indian Health Board	107
Instituto de Arte y Cultura	22
Insurance Brokers of Minnesota	91
Interact Center for the Visual and Performing Arts	119
Intermedia Arts	4, 73, 78
International Documentary Association	44, 104
International Sculpture Center	37, 105
Internet ArtResources	31
Irish Music & Dance Association	23

J

Jerome Foundation	74
Jewish Community Center of Greater Minneapolis	23
Jewish Community Center of the Greater St. Paul Area	23
John Michael Kohler Arts Center	17, 78
JuxtaPosition Arts	4, 27

L

La Prensa de Minnesota	25
Lake Country Pastel Society	35
Lake Region Arts Council (Region 4)	12, 76
Legal Aid Society of Minnesota	99
Loft Literary Center, The	66, 74
Lotta Theatrical Fund	85
Lutheran Social Service of Minnesota - Credit Counseling Service	90

M

MacPhail Center for the Arts	27, 56
MacRostie Art Center	18
MAP for Nonprofits	4, 91
McKnight Foundation, The	74
Medical Assistance - Hennepin County	107
Medical Assistance - Ramsey County	108
Metropolitan Council	80
Metropolitan Regional Arts Council (Region 11)	15
Midwest Art Fairs Directory	5, 48
Midwest Media Artists Access Center	44
Migizi – National Native Information Center	47
Minneapolis American Indian Center/Two Rivers Gallery	18, 24
Minneapolis College of Art and Design	27
Minneapolis Community Development Agency	79, 81, 102
Minneapolis Department of Health and Family Support	108
Minneapolis Drum and Dance Center	57
Minneapolis Foundation, The	85
Minneapolis Handbook of the Streets	115

M cont.

Minneapolis Office of Cultural Affairs - Film, Video, Recording & New Media	44
Minneapolis Tenant's Union	102
Minneapolis Writers' Workshop	66
Minnesota AIDS Project	110
Minnesota Alliance for Arts in Education	28, 97
Minnesota Artist Association	7, 34
Minnesota Art Therapy Association	8, 112
Minnesota Artists Exhibition Program	34
Minnesota Association for Music Therapy	57, 112
Minnesota Association of Community Theatres	61
Minnesota Association of Songwriters	57
Minnesota Ballet	63
Minnesota Basket Weavers Guild	51
Minnesota Bluegrass and Old-time Music Association	58
MinnesotaCare	105
Minnesota Cartoonists League	36
Minnesota Center for Book Arts (MCBA)	70, 78
Minnesota Chapter of the Gospel Music Workshop	58
Minnesota Childcare Resource and Referral Network	121
Minnesota Citizens for the Arts	97
Minnesota Comprehensive Health Association	105
Minnesota Contemporary Quilters	51
Minnesota Council on Foundations	75
Minnesota Crafts Council	49
Minnesota Dance Alliance	64
Minnesota Dance Theatre & School	64
Minnesota Department of Revenue	92, 95
Minnesota Department of Transportation	95

M cont.

Minnesota Film Board	45
Minnesota Guitar Society	58
Minnesota Housing Finance Agency	81, 102
Minnesota Knitters' Guild	51
Minnesota Lace Society	52
Minnesota Literature	67, 75
Minnesota Music Academy	58
Minnesota Music Directory	59
Minnesota Public Utilities Commission	113
Minnesota Quilters, Inc.	52
Minnesota River School of Fine Art	28
Minnesota Society of Children's Book Writers and Illustrators	42, 67
Minnesota State Arts Board	11, 28, 75
Minnesota State Bar Association Attorney Referral Service	99
Minnesota State Services for the Blind	119
Minnesota Therapeutic Massage Network	112
Minnesota Valley Action Council	81
Minnesota Valley Fiber Arts Guild	52
Minnesota Watercolor Society	36
Minnesota Women's Press, The	25
Minnesota Wood Carvers' Association	38
Minnesota Woodturners Association	39
Minnesota Woodworkers Guild	39
Minnetonka Center for the Arts	18
John Munger	92
MusiCares Foundation	86
Musician's Assistance Program	59, 116

N

National Art Education Association	28
National Artists Equity Association	97, 105
National Association of Artist's Organizations (NAAO)	8
National Association for Poetry Therapy (NAPT)	67, 113
National Association for the Self-Employed	8, 98
National Association of Women Artists, Inc.	9
National Endowment for the Arts	75
National Foundation for Advancement of the Arts	75
National Sculpture Society	37, 76, 105
National Writers Union	67, 105
Needlework Guild of Minnesota	52
Neighborhood Health Care Network	108
Neighborhood Revitalization Program	102
New York Artists Equity Association, Inc. (NYAEA)	98, 99
New York Mills Arts Retreat & Regional Cultural Center	78
No Name Exhibitions	5
Nobles County Art Center	18
Northeast Minneapolis Arts Association	9
Northern Clay Center	49
Northlands Storytelling Network	65
Northstar Watercolor Society	36
Northwest Regional Arts Council (Region1)	11

O

Occupational Health Services	111
Office of Cultural Affairs: Minneapolis Arts	30
Origins Program	29
Outfront Minnesota	116

P

pARTS Photographic Arts	46
Pathways	113
P.E.N. Fund for Writers and Editors with HIV/AIDS	76, 110
P.E.N. Writers Fund	68, 86
Percussive Arts Society, Minnesota Chapter	59, 105
Pillsbury House	19
Planned Parenthood of Minnesota	108
Playwrights' Center, The	62, 68, 76, 78
Pollock-Krasner Foundation, Inc.	76
Prairie Lakes Regional Arts Council (Region 9)	14, 77
Professional Photographers of America	46
Public Art St. Paul	31

R

Ramsey Action Programs for Washington County	86
Ramsey Action Programs, Inc.	114
Region 2 Arts Council	12
Resources and Counseling for the Arts	79, 87, 92, 93, 99
ReUse Center	34
Rimon Jewish Metropolitan Council on Arts and Culture	24
Rochester Art Center	19

S

Sage Women's Clinic	109
St. Paul Art Collective	5
St. Paul Arts Partnership	5
St. Paul Housing Information Office	103
St. Paul Needleworkers Guild	53

S cont.

St. Paul Planning and Economic Development	79, 81, 103
Salvation Army Heat / Share (Minneapolis)	114
Salvation Army Heat / Share (Ramsey County)	114
SASE: The Write Place	68
Screen Actors Guild (SAG)	62
Screenwriters Workshop	69
Sculptor.Org	38
Second Harvest St. Paul Food Bank	117
Sexual Offense Services of Ramsey County	116
Siggraph	42
Southeastern Minnesota Arts Council (Region 10)	15
Southwest Minnesota Arts & Humanities Council (Regions 6E, 6W, 8)	13
Space: A Basic Guide to Performance and Rehearsal Spaces in Minnesota	6
Storyfront	65
Studio, The	29, 34

T

Tax Clinic	93
Textile Center of Minnesota	53
Textile Council of the Minneapolis Institute of Arts	54
Theater Communications Group	62
Twin Cities Jazz Society	60
Twin Cities Musicians Union	60, 98, 105
Twin Cities Neighborhood Housing	103
Twin Cities Women's Art Show Collective	6
TwinCitiesArtists.com	48

Index – U-W

U

United States Copyright Office	96
United States Patent & Trademark Office	96
United States Small Business Administration	80
United Way First Call for Help – Minneapolis Branch	82, 93, 116
United Way First Call for Help – St. Paul Branch	82, 93, 116
University Film Society	45
University of Minnesota School of Dentistry	109
Upper Midwest Bead Society	54
Upper Midwest Conservation Association	9
Upper Mississippi Blues Society	60
USDA, Rural Development	82

V

Village Family Service Center, The	91, 93
Vision Quest Photographic Arts Center	46, 78
Visual Artist Information Hotline	35
Volunteer Lawyer's Network	100
VSA Arts of Minnesota	120

W

Waseca Art Center	19
Watson/Ragmala Dance Center	64
Weavers' Guild and School of Minnesota	54
West Bank School of Music	29, 60
Women in Photography and Visual Arts	35, 47
Women Photographers and Visual Artists (WPVA)	47

W cont.

Women's Art Registry of Minnesota (WARM)	10
Women's Caucus for Art	106
Women's and Children's Health Programs	109
Women Venture	88
Wood Carving Store and School, The	39
Wooden Cove, The	40

Y

Young Audiences of Minnesota	29

Z

Zenon Dance Company and School	64

Law of Art—Art of Law

Robert P. Abdo   Kenneth J. Abdo   Daniel M. Satorius   Timothy C. Matson

ATTORNEYS AT LAW

Est. 1936

Practitioners of Entertainment Law

Including music, film, video, talent, media and business representation
Contracts, securities and litigation

710 Northstar West • 625 Marquette Avenue • Minneapolis, MN 55402

Phone (612) 333-1526   Fax (612) 342-2608

www.abdoabdo.com

THINK OPPENHEIMER

PROTECTING CREATIVE ASSETS

Oppenheimer's Intellectual Property Group is in the business of protecting creative ideas like yours in Minnesota and around the world. When you think of protecting your creative assets, THINK OPPENHEIMER.

Ernest Grumbles 612.607.7503

OPPENHEIMER WOLFF & DONNELLY LLP

oppenheimer.com
888.269.3529

■ Amsterdam ■ Brussels ■ Chicago ■ Geneva
■ Los Angeles ■ Minneapolis ■ New York
■ Orange County ■ Paris ■ Saint Paul
■ Silicon Valley ■ Washington, D.C.

FISH & RICHARDSON P.C., P.A.

Boston
Delaware
New York
San Diego
Silicon Valley
Twin Cities
Washington, DC

Artists and arts adminstrators, are you facing copyright and trademark questions?

Fish & Richardson serves clients in the fine and performing arts. Please call Stephen Baird at 612 335-5070.

Intellectual property and technology law

www.fr.com

Shhhhhhhhhhh...

The very things you talk about the least may be what you need to protect the most. You certainly don't want to find your most valuable assets in your competitor's pocket: your revolutionary invention at a former employee's new company...your distinctive logo design slightly altered by a rival firm. Our **Intellectual Property Group** can help you establish, preserve and protect your patents, trademarks, copyrights and trade secrets. Be smart about your intellectual property. Your success may be at stake. *Let us keep your secrets.*

RIDER BENNETT EGAN & ARUNDEL

A Limited Liability Partnership

333 South Seventh Street   Suite 2000   Minneapolis, MN 55402   (612) 340-7951   Fax: (612) 340-7890
email: info@riderlaw.com   Web site: www.riderlaw.com

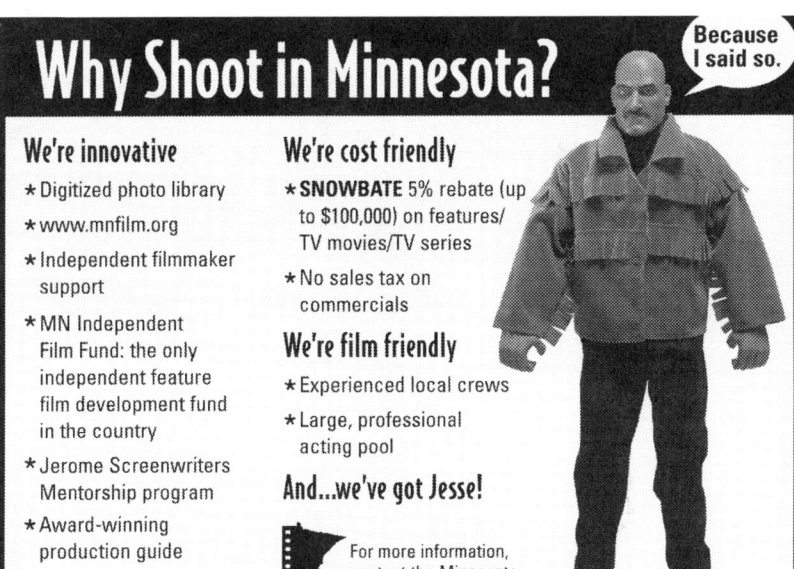

Why Shoot in Minnesota?

Because I said so.

We're innovative
* Digitized photo library
* www.mnfilm.org
* Independent filmmaker support
* MN Independent Film Fund: the only independent feature film development fund in the country
* Jerome Screenwriters Mentorship program
* Award-winning production guide

We're cost friendly
* **SNOWBATE** 5% rebate (up to $100,000) on features/TV movies/TV series
* No sales tax on commercials

We're film friendly
* Experienced local crews
* Large, professional acting pool

And...we've got Jesse!

For more information, contact the Minnesota Film Board at 612.332.6493 or info@mnfilm.org

---

COMPACT DISC MANUFACTURING & GRAPHIC DESIGN SERVICES

612.788.1659

WWW.NOISELAND.COM

NOISELAND INDUSTRIES

Serving the Legal Needs of Creative Professionals

Kenneth L. Kunkle
Attorney at Law

612-414-3113

Contract Review and Drafting
Small Business Issues
Copyright and Trademark
Estate Planning

www.KunkleLaw.com

Handbook for Minnesota Artists – 141

No one understands your business like someone who's been in it.

Advertising, Communications & Entertainment Law Group

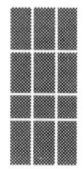

FREDRIKSON & BYRON, P.A.
Attorneys and Advisors

(612) 347-7000   www.fredlaw.com

Passion

You've Got It. We've Got It. Let's Talk.

Our Business Practice Attorneys represent Entertainment Industry Clients from Individual Artists, Entrepreneurs and Start-up Businesses to Multi-million Dollar Corporations, their Officers, Shareholders and Talent.

Spence Olson P.L.L.C.
Let Our Talent Protect Your Talent

Copyright Registration & Litigation • Recording and Management Contracts • Breach of Contract
Entrepreneurial Assistance for Emerging Companies • Partnership/Corporate Disputes
Contract Review and Negotiation • Defamation, Publicity & Privacy Matters

For your <u>FREE</u> initial consultation, contact Mick Spence at (612) 339-9121 or mspence@meshbesher.com
1616 Park Avenue Minneapolis, MN • www.meshbesher.com

The Arts & Entertainment Law Section of the Minnesota State Bar Association

Officers

Chair: Mick Spence
Treasurer: Julie Moore
Vice-Chair: Cami Ruhland
Secretary: Michael Fleming

Section Members

Kenneth J. Abdo
Robert P. Abdo
Jon O. Ahlberg
Melinda A. Aurandt
Leonard Axelrod
Stephen R. Baird
John L. Beard
Martin Berg
Rebecca J. Bishop
Joseph R. Borman
Felicia J. Boyd
Michael J. Bradley
Lee M. Brennan
Betsey D. Buckheit
Joshua J. Burke
Laurel Graham Burke
Christopher A. Camardello
Andrew M. Carlson
Mitchel C. Chargo
Michelle L. Clark
Steven C. Clay
Matthew D. Clementson
John A. Clifford
Mary Jo Ruff Cole
Richard J. Coleman
Benjamin Coler
Timothy C. Cook
Gayle L. Crose
Michelle T. Culligan
Peter J. Culp
Christopher T. Curry
Mark E. Czuchry
Laura J. Danielson
Frederick R. Dawe
Charles H. De La Garza
Michael K. De Kruif
Victoria S. Dennis
Leah M. DiOrio
Tina M. Dobbelaere
Eduardo E. Drake
Diane L. Drays
Ann Dunn Wessberg
Galen W. Eagle Bull
Brad C. Eggen
Anthony T. Eliseuson
Sandra Epp Ryan
James T. Erickson
Amy E. Erskine
Michael F. Fleming
Michael Freske
Melissa B. Garlington
Christina M. Garner
Barbara J. Gislason
Gregory C. Golla
Barbara J. Grahn
Mitzi T. Gramling
Michael J. Grimes
Ernest W. Grumbles
Michael S. Grundstrom
Marc S. Gurstel
James E. Haase
Sten E. Hakanson

Mark C. Halverson
April M. Hamlin
Curtis B. Hamre
Todd G. Hartman
Kyle R. Hartnett
Jennifer Hartzell
Thomas A. Hassing
Michelle M. Hayes
Britt Heglund
Craig K. Hemphill
Deanna L. Henshaw
Alfred C. Holden
Michael W. Hubbard
Robert F. Ihinger
Scott N. Ihrig
Naomi D. Isaacson
Ryan S. Johnson
Whitney L. Joondeph
Patrick M. Kelley
William R. Kennedy
John T. Knight
David W. Koehser
Jacquelyn A. Kozak
Kenneth L. Kunkle
Dollene L. Lamberto
Michael A. Landrum
Paul L. Landry
Richard A. Latterell
Laurel E. Learmonth
Paul A. Ledford
Stephen C. Lee
Barbara J. Lefky
James M. Lehman
John C. Levy
Calvin L. Litsey
Bruce H. Little
James D. Lockhart
Mark D. Malloy
Brian M. Marsden
Mary K. Martin
Jody Martineau
Nancy V. L. Mate
Timothy C. Matson
Daniel W. McDonald
Joy S. McGinnis
Michael J. McGuire
James C. Melville
Jeffrey M. Melville
Jessica B. Merz
Robert S. Metcalf
Ryan G. Miest
Julie A. Moore
Yvonne B. Moore
Aaron S. Mowrey
Adam M. Nathe
Donald W. Niles
Diane M. Odeen
Kevin P. O'Laughlin
Debra Kass Orenstein
Michael A. Perelstein
Michael G. Phillips
James R. Pielemeier

Denise Plachecki
Randi Pollack
Alan W. Porter
John W. Provo
David W. Quist
Peter L. Radosevich
Rae L. Randolph
Michael J. Riehm
Rachel A. Riensche
Jessica B. Rivas
Theodore Roberts
Walter Roseau
John D. Rosteck
Linda Alsid Ruehle
Cami J. Ruhland
Alan K. Ruvelson
Robin A. Sannes
Daniel M. Satorius
Thomas K. Scallen
Tami L. Schroeder
Gregory A. Sebald
Sandra M. Sedo
James B. Sheehy
Lee E. Sheehy
Maximillian Shemesh
Philip L. Sieff
Nancy L. Skovran
Andrew Sloss
Stephanie J. Smith
Chyara P. Smith-Stopp
Michael B. Sonsteng
Russell M. Spence
Susan H. Stephan
John H. Stout
Sylvia L. Strobel
Gretchen R. Strong
Matthew J. Sund
Christina A. Svalstad
Richard A. Swartz
Gregory R. Tambornino
Timothy J. Teichgraeber
Cheri Templeman
Jill J. Theis
Joseph K. Thiegs
Jeffrey K. Thomas
Diane A. Thompson
Douglas M. Thorpe
Daniel R. Tyson
Gillian B. Uecker
John T. Wendt
David C. West
Ralf D. Wiedemann
Thomas Brown Wiese
Nancy J. Wigchers
Fawn E. Wilderson
Lundy J. Windeck
Stephen Winnick
Mark D. Wisser
Timothy M. Wong
Stacy A. Woods
Barry M. Zelickson

Tax preparation, financial planning, and business organization for artists, musicians, and other self employed creative people.

BEGLEY LAW OFFICES, P.A.
12 SOUTH SIXTH STREET, SUITE 1040, MINNEAPOLIS, MN 55402
(612)333-7530 TEL.   (612) 333-5462 FAX.

Saint Paul

Founded in 1849. Rediscovered in 2000

The City of Saint Paul understands the value of the arts and culture. With more than 100 arts organizations, 3000 full-time jobs, and 3.6 million visitors drawn to the city by cultural organizations annually, we know supporting the arts is a great investment.

We will promote your next performance in Saint Paul, advise you on funding options, or find a location for your film shoot. We're here to help.

Jeff Nelson
Director of Cultural Development
City of Saint Paul, 1300 CHA
Saint Paul, MN 55102

(651) 266-6560

Leah Otto
Film Liaison
City of Saint Paul, 170 CH
Saint Paul, MN 55102

(651) 266-6646

www.ci.stpaul.mn.us

Notes

Handbook for Minnesota Artists

Tear–Out Order Form

Use this simple form to order more copies of RCA's *Handbook for Minnesota Artists*. Remember, if you purchase more than 5 copies, you save $3.50 per copy. Make checks out to RCA.
Mail orders to: RCA, 308 Prince St., Suite 270, St. Paul, MN 55101.

Name: _____

Address: _____

City: _____ State: _____ Zip: _____

— Send me the *Handbook:*   copies: _____ @ $12

 Shipping: _____ @ $2 each

— Send me 5 or more *Handbooks*:   copies: _____ @ $8.50

 Shipping: _____ @ $2 each

TOTAL AMOUNT ENCLOSED: _____